# THE
# FIRST JAPANESE MISSION
## TO
# AMERICA
## (1860)

SR Scholarly Resources Inc.
Wilmington, Delaware

SCHOLARLY RESOURCES, INC.
1508 Pennsylvania Avenue
Wilmington, Delaware 19806


Reprint edition published in 1973
First published in 1937 by J. L. Thompson & Co.,
    Japan

Reprinted from the Collection of
Ohio State University Libraries


Library of Congress Catalog Card Number: 72-82119
ISBN: 0-8420-1412-8


Manufactured in the United States of America

# THE
# FIRST JAPANESE MISSION
## TO
# AMERICA
## (1860)

### Being a Diary Kept by a Member
### of the Embassy

*Translated into English by*

JUNICHI FUKUYAMA & RODERICK H. JACKSON

*Edited with an Introduction by*

M. G. MORI

❧

J. L. THOMPSON & CO., (RETAIL) LTD.,
Kobe, Japan.

1937

# INTRODUCTION

This Diary of a Voyage, translated into English for the first time by Mr. Fukuyama Jun-ichi and Mr. Roderick H. Jackson in 1933, is as far as I know the most complete one of the five extant journals of the official mission sent to America by the Shogunal Government of Japan in 1860 (the first year of Man-yen). Similar missions were also sent by the Shogunate to Russia, England, the Netherlands, Spain, and other countries of Europe, but the one despatched to the United States is of peculiar interest to us today not only because of the predominant rôle played by America in the Europeanization of Japan in its initial stages, but also because of the very full account of the mission still available, being indeed more detailed and entertaining than that of any other official party sent abroad in those days.

The Author of the Diary is Yanagawa Masakiyo, one of the chief retainers of Niimi Masaoki, Shogunal High Commissioner for Foreign Affairs, who had just been appointed head of the deputation. This embassy, which consisted of 93 men, included Katsu Kaishū, Fukuzawa Yukichi, and Nakahama Manjirō—men whose names will long remain in Japanese history as pioneers in the modernization of the country and its people. In the previous year the American Government had sent to the port of Uraga (at the mouth of Yedo Bay) the frigate *Powhatan* (2415 tons), with an invitation to the Shogunal Government to despatch a deputation for the purpose of observing actual conditions in America and exchanging ratification for a treaty of commerce between the two countries. The party set sail from Uraga on the 22nd of January, 1860 (lunar calendar). The *Powhatan*, with Niimi Masaoki and most of his suite on board, was guarded by the Japanese warship *Kanrin-Maru* with Admiral Katsu in command. The voyage turned out to be an unusually rough one, the American pilot declaring that he had never experienced the like of it on the Pacific before. The party landed at Honolulu, and paid a visit to the royal palace there, where they were most cordially entertained. They reached San Francisco on the 9th of March, left the *Kanrin-Maru* there, and sailed down the coast in the *Powhatan* as far as Panama, where they disembarked and crossed the isthmus to the Atlantic coast in a "land-steamer," that is, a train ! That was their first railway journey. From Panama they sailed up the coast to New York, from whence they were taken in a newly-built riverboat up to Washington, D. C. They arrived in the National Capital on the 25th of April and three days later paid a formal visit to the White House, to present the Shogun's official message to President Buchanan. On the third of May they exchanged ratifications with the U. S. Secretary of State for the first treaty of commerce between Japan and America, thus successfully accomplishing their primary mission.

They then "did" the sights of such leading American towns as Baltimore, Philadelphia, and New York, and left the last-named city on board the *Niagara*, then the largest warship of the U. S. Navy, on the 13th of June. The *Niagara* with the party on board, rounded Cape Horn, touched at St. Vincent in the British West Indies, Loanda in South Africa, Batavia and Hong Kong, and at last cast anchor off Shinagawa on the 28th of September. Niimi and his suite, who had thus completed their long and arduous journey round the world, were received in audience by the Shogun on the 29th day of the same month.

The first year of Man-yen (1860), in which Niimi and his men carried out this memorable cruise, was made still more memorable by a great fire in Yedo and by the assasination of Ii Naosuke outside the Sakurada Gate by a band of anti-foreign rōnin from Mito. The next year, the first year of Bunkyū, saw further anti-foreign demonstrations by Mito men, including an attack on the British legation at Takanawa. The Shogunate, however, remained firm in its policy of friendly dealings with Western powers, allowing them to build legations at Shinagawa. Anti-Western outbursts continued in the second year of Bunkyū (1862), when the British legation at Shinagawa was set on fire, American and Dutch warships fired on, and so forth. But the same year a group of students were sent to Holland for study, and other measures taken in accordance with the same policy. Events moved rapidly, and we find Fukuzawa Yukichi, one of Niimi's embassy, founding in the third year of Keio (1867) his private school which has since grown more prosperous each year, until it is now one of the most influential educational establishments in the country, and is known as Keio University. By that time the

Imperial Court itself had given the Shogunate formal permission to conclude treaties with European nations, and students had been sent to England and other countries with a view to the introduction of Western learning into Japan. When, therefore, the Emperor Meiji ascended the throne in 1867, his highest advisers recommended the formal opening of the Empire to foreign intercourse, and Hyōgo (now better known as Kōbe) was declared an open port. The detailed reports of conditions in the West brought home by Niimi and others sent to America and Europe may not have had immediate effects on the foreign policy of Japan as a whole, but they certainly helped the Shogunate officials to form a fairly correct opinion of the world situation at that crucial point in the nation's history and to guide its foreign policy as wisely as the difficult political situation allowed them.

It would be too much to expect an English translation (however faithfully executed) to do full justice to the original Japanese of the diary, which is in the (to us) somewhat quaint literary style of the later Tokugawa period ; but the translators have, as far as circumstances allowed, striven to reproduce every entry and statement in the journal, so that the English version may be looked upon as of nearly equal documentary value with the Japanese original as a record of the doings of the mission and of their observation of American institutions and contemporary events. The diarist, for instance, discusses certain features of the American constitutional system of government, describes American manners and customs from a Japanese point of view, relates the circumstances of a visit to the home of Commodore Perry (then, alas ! no longer living), and gives us vivid pictures of some cultural, social, and religious institutions of that country, as well as of the enthusiastic, not to say royal, welcome they received wherever they went. If the sentiments of admiration and gratitude expressed by him in this journal (never intended for a white man's perusal) should help to cement still further the peaceful relations that have since existed between the two Pacific nations—relations at times sorely tested and even clouded, but never broken—the labours of all concerned in the publication of this English translation will have been more than amply rewarded.

*October 18th, 1937.*                    MASATOSHI GENSEN MORI.

# THE AUTHOR'S PREFACE

In the first year of the Man-yen era, on the 18th day of the first month (January 18, 1860), we started on our mission to the United States of America in accordance with official instructions previously received. From Kudan Hill we proceeded to the Tsukiji military training school at Kamakuragashi - Nihonbashidori. There we had a roll-call and partook of lunch together at noon, after which we went into large fishing-vessels, which carried us to the *Powhatan*, the American ship which had been sent to convey us across the waters. She weighed anchor without delay, proceeded to the port of Yokohama, and cast anchor there for a few days' stay. The following day (19th) Lord Sakai, of Iki Province, and Lord Akamatsu-Saemonnojo, Shogunal officers in charge of foreign affairs; Lord Takemoto, Shogunal Secretary for Education; and Lord Jimbo, of Hōki Province, Superintendent of Police, came on board to bid us farewell. On the 22nd we set sail from Yokohama, and the journal of our voyage from the next day follows.

# CONTENTS

## ILLUSTRATIONS

# DIARY OF VOYAGE

## Volume I

January 18 (luner calender), 1860.  Clear.  Evening West Wind.

In the morning at eleven o'clock we set out from Kudanzaka, Tokyo, and went to a military training camp in Tsukiji, Tokyo. There we assembled and ate lunch.  In the afternoon we embarked in a large fishing boat and, sailing about seven miles, we passed by the forts and arrived at the American war-ship Powhatan, which had come from the United States to take us on our voyage.

When we went on board about one o'clock there was a welcoming salute of 21 guns according to the American custom.  The anchor was raised immediately, and sailing southwest about 20 miles we arrived off Yokohama about 2:30 p.m.  There we cast anchor and spent the night enjoying a banquet until one o'clock in the morning.

This boat was large, but the space assigned the Japanese commission seemed small.  Our quarters were below deck, and in the four sides of our rooms there were two tiers of bunks  There were seven rooms and in each there were eleven persons.  The width of the bunks was two feet and the length was more than six feet. There was a rail about six inches high along the side of the bunks to keep the occupant from falling out in his sleep.

This ship is a frigate, and in America is called a warship. When the Americans first came to Japan in 1853 it is said that Commodore Perry was on this ship.

The length of this ship was 300 feet, the width was 54 feet, and she carried 24 guns.  The war complement is 800 men and several hundred rifles, it is said.  This ship has four decks and eleven ladders leading from one deck to another.  The Captain's room was on the top deck in the rear.  The rooms of the other officers were on both sides of the ship.

The kitchen for the Japanese was in the middle of the ship and that of the Americans was next to it.  The chairman of the Japanese commission had his bedroom in the rear of the second deck. Forward from this cabin was a large reception room about 30x45 ft. The floor was covered by a carpet with flower design and the walls were decorated with a large mirror and several pictures, the effect of which was very beautiful. Next to this hall was the room of the lieutenant. Underneath was the main dining room. On the dining room floor was a carpet like that of the reception room. There was a fine dining room table 24 feet long, 9 feet wide and a little more than 3 feet high. The large quarters for the sailors were forward from the dining room and being crowded reminded us of the rooms in which the servants of the "samurai" live. The engine room was in the middle of this deck. Forward and to the rear of the engine room were the storage rooms. And on the second deck above the storage rooms below were storage rooms for vegetables, coal, rum, rice, wood, water, and other provisions. The remaining description of the ship I leave to your imagination.

January 19, 1860.          Clear.          West Wind.

We spent the day at anchor. About noon the Japanese Secretary for Foreign Affairs, Sakai Okinokami, and the Under Secretary for Foreign Affairs, Akamatsu Saemonnojo, and the Secretary for Education, Takemoto, and the Chief of Metropolitan Police, Jimbo Hokinokami, came to bid us good-by. They returned about 2 P.M.

January 20, 1860.          Cloudy.          North Wind.

While we were anchored in the harbour the American soldiers drilled each day on deck with rifles. About noon a notice was posted as follows:

1. Smoking is forbidden except in the guard room.
2. Paper lanterns are forbidden on ship board.
3. Lights out at 10 P.M. except in guard room.
4. Fire is forbidden in cabins.
5. American kitchen to be closed a little after 8 P.M.
   Japanese      „    „  „      „   at 8 P.M.
6. It is forbidden to give "sake" (wine) to the crew.
7. One gallon of water is allowed daily per person for cooking.
8. Tongs, etc. should not be kept in the rooms after being used.

9. Because of fire hazard beware of lamps.

10. Officers only are allowed in the guard room.

11. Senior grade officers use toilet on right.

Junior ,, ,, ,, ,, ,, left.

All others use toilet in prow.

12. If there is any difficulty between the Japanese and the crew notify the First Lieutenant through the interpretrer.

13. The above orders having been issued by the Captain let us obey them.

January 21, 1860.          Cloudy.          North Wind.

Today the ship is at anchor. About noon it began snowing. One sailor became sick and died on board. From 8:00 A.M. to 4:00 P.M. one shot is fired each hour if the commander is on board.

January 22, 1860.          Clear.          Rain at Mid-Night.
                                           North Wind.

Before 10:00 A.M. we raised anchor and sailed out of Yokohama harbour in a southerly direction. After 10 o'clock we passed Uraga (the place where Commodore Perry landed.). About 11 o'clock we sighted Izu Peninsula on the right. Then we changed our course to the East. We sighted a Japanese man-of-war proceeding from Nagasaki to Yokohama, and an American merchant ship entering Yokohama harbour. Both of these ships blew their whistles as we passed. The waves became high and the boat rolled and pitched so that we retired. But we wished to see the mountains of Japan before we were out of sight, so we again went up on deck, but after a little while we went below again. Only a very few of the Japanese were able to eat lunch. We were told that we would pass Choshi and Nambu during the night.

From the entrance of Yokohama bay to Boshu is 40 miles. One American mile is 17 cho 14 ken.

Position North Latitude 38° 50' 40"

Position East Longitude 139° 50' 10"

Temperature 49° F.

January 23, 1860.          Severe Northwest Wind.

In the afternoon there was a severe storm. Today we could see neither islands nor mountains, nothing except the vast sea. From noon yesterday until noon today we travelled 178 miles.

Latitude     N. 35° 20′ 46″
Longitude    E. 140° 10′ 10″
Temperature 48° F.

January 24, 1860.     Morning West Wind.   Afternoon East Wind.

Although we are on the great ocean we have music morning and evening. We have this music because all is well. The sailors drill with guns. About eleven o'clock an officer wearing a saber calls the roll and gives each sailor a cup of beer. The beer is yellow and bitter. The cup which is used is made of tin and contains about ½ pint. The crew is forbidden to drink beer without permission but the officers are at liberty to drink. From noon yesterday until noon today we have sailed 200 miles.

Latitude     N. 35° 17′ 40″
Longitude    E. 148° 17′ 40″
Temperature 50° F.

January 25, 1860.          Clear.          Northwest wind severe.
                                           A little rain.

We are proceeding Northeast. The sailors drill. Today there is music both morning and evening. The music today is different. Usually there are nine musicians but today the flute and drum being added there are eleven. From noon yesterday until noon today we sailed 204 miles.

Latitude     N. 35° 54′ 59″.
Longitude    E. 151° 17′ 45″.
Temperature 43° F.

January 26, 1860.          Clear.          East wind.

The waves are calm. The rolling and pitching of the ship is less. The feeling of the Japanese has greatly improved. There are many birds about the size of a pigeon on the water. They have black feathers and white rings around their eyes. Though we are in the midst of the ocean it is not raining. Because there is drill and music daily I will not record it henceforth. From noon yesterday until noon today we covered 225 miles.

Latitude     N. 35° 51′ 29″.
Longitude   E. 155° 40′.
Temperature 50° F.

January 27, 1860.     Severe South wind.  Storm in the evening.

In the morning the waves were high and the ship rolled and pitched. In the evening there was wind and rain. The angry waves washed over the deck of the ship. The deck looked like a raging river and there was a noice like thunder. The waves looked like great mountains and valleys. The ship rose to heaven and fell to earth, and the small furniture and decorations flew about like feathers. The lamps went out and the ship was in complete darkness. An officer commanded the crew and we heard the sound of his voice, but I am unable to write what he said. The Japanese were unable to walk about. When necessary we walked with the assistance of the Americans. The Americans worked as usual even while the ship rolled and pitched. Following the commands of the officer the sailors brought the ship safely through the storm. A large wave washed over the deck and carried away one life boat which was fastened by iron chains. Two feet of the side of the ship was torn away and the raging waves dashed in and wet our bed clothing and swords, causing us great anxiety. We were so sick and miserable that we had no strength to repair the hole in the side of the ship. The waves washed into the room where I was, wetting our wicker baskets in which our clothes were packed. I lay very weak and miserable in my bunk, unable to do anything. From yesterday noon until today noon we sailed 190 miles.

Latitude     N. 36° 23′ 39″.
Longitude   E. 159° 28′.
Temperature 58° F.

January 28, 1860.    Rain.    Severe West Wind. Direction East by Northeast.

This morning, though there was wind and rain, it was much calmer than yesterday. We were greatly relieved. There were many places about the ship which were damaged by the storm. The Japanese kitchen was wrecked. By evening it had been repaired and we all ate supper. The Captain said it was the worst storm he had experienced in forty years. He said that if the ship had been a regular merchant boat it would have been destroyed but that because it was an American warship we were saved. He said it was regrettable for any counry's warship to lose a life-boat. In the evening the wind and rain ceased so that we felt that we had been raised from the dead by the help of heaven. Day's run 154 miles.

Latitude　　　N. 36° 48′ 33″.
Longitude　　E. 163° 34′.
Temperature 56° F.

January 29, 1860.　　　A little cloudy.　　　North Wind.
　　　　　　　　　　　　　　　　　　　　　　Direction—Northeast.

Day's run 208 miles.
Latitude　　　N. 35° 58′ 42″.
Longitude　　E. 166° 45′ 10″.
Temperature 56° F.

January 30 1860.　　　A little cloudy.　　　East Wind.

Today there was an inspection. Immediately after the beating of the drum and blowing of the whistle all the crew came up on deck. The Captain, accompanied by a Lieutenant wearing a sword, came on deck. Soldiers carrying guns, ship carpenters with their tools, and sailors lined up. The Lieutenant called the roll. When the drum was beaten each man returned to his work. Day's run 181 miles.

Latitude　　　N. 35° 33′ 25″.
Longitude　　E. 170° 21′ 33″.
Temperature 55° F.

February 1st.　　　Rain.　　　Severe West Wind.

We sailed in an Eastern direction. As today is Washington's birthday there was a gun salute. In the evening a banquet was scheduled but it was cancelled on account of stormy weather. Because of the storm the ship rolled and pitched. The sailors were given a reward of $ 1,000.00 because of their good work during the storm on the 27th. The value of the dollar is three " Bu." (Note : " Bu " is the name of money used in Japan in the middle of the 19th century), Day's run 165 miles.

Latitude     N. 36° 30' 55".
Longitude   E. 173° 33' 03".
Temperature 54° F.

February 2nd.          Cloudy.       West Wind.
Rain in afternoon.
Direction: East by Northeast. Day's run 220 miles.
    Latitude     N. 37° 51'.
    Longitude   E. 177° 36' 15".
    Temperature 48½° F.

February 3rd.       Cloudy—Fair.     Northeast Wind.

Because the storm on the first interferred with the George Washington birthday celebration it was held today. The officers went into their dining room and had a banquet consisting of cherry brandy, chicken, pork, beef, mutton and other delicacies. The sailors also had wine and meat and held a jolly banquet. Day's run 220 miles.
    Latitude     N. 37° 55' 32".
    Longitude   E. 177° 50' 45".
    Temperature 50° F.

February 4th.          Clear.         North Wind.

Direction Northeast.
    Latitude     N. 38° 1' 36".
    Longitude   W. 170° 36' 30".
    Temperature 55° F.

February 5th.          Clear.       Northeast Wind.

Day's run 200 miles.
    Latitude     N. 38° 4' 30".
    Longitude   W. 169° 31' 30".
    Temperature 52° F.

February 6th.          Clear.       Northeast Wind.

    Calm sea. After 12 o'clock the whistle was blown and the drum sounded. All the sailors assembled on deck. The captain stood in the middle of the deck and gave instructions. All who heard him removed their caps. After the captain finished giving his instructions the drum sounded and all the sailors returned to their posts. The sailors drink beer six or seven times in ten days. The decks are scrubbed three or four times in one month. The roll is called three or four times every ten days. Every one must abide by these rules. Since these things are done regularly by rule I shall not mention them again. Day's run, 182 miles.

Latitude    N. 38° 21' 12".
Longitude    W. 165° 48' 15".
Temperature 53° F.

February 7th.                Cloudy.                Northeast Wind.

From noon the ship headed south toward the Sandwich Islands. Because of strong head winds there was not enough coal to make the trip to San Frencisco in California, therefore we put into the Sandwich Islands. Day's run 209 miles.

Latitude    N. 35° 25' 52".
Longitude    W. 161° 17' 20".
Temperature 59° F.

February 9th.                Rain.                East Wind.

Direction :   South by Southeast.

It has become sultry since the day before yesterday, it is remarked. The speed of the ship was retarded by head winds. Each day we see the birds, but have seen nothing else of interest. Day's run 172 miles.

Latitude    N. 33° 11' 11".
Longitude    W. 160° 37'.
Temperature 65° F.

February 10th.                Cloudy.                Southeast Wind.

Direction :   South. Day's run 162 miles.

Latitude    N. 30° 21' 40".
Longitude    W. 159° 44' 13".
Temperature 65° F.

February 11th.                  Fair—Cloudy.                  East Wind.

Direction: South by Southeast.  Day's run 110 miles.
    Latitude        N. 18° 34' 53".
    Longitude       W. 160° 12' 45".
    Temperature 70° F.


February 12th.                  Little Rain.                  Severe East Wind.

Because of severe East wind a yard was broken.  The drinking water became yellow so that the boiled rice looked like rice cooked in tea.  Day's run 158 miles.
    Latitude        N. 26° 11' 58".
    Longitude       W. 159° 37' 51".
    Temperature 72° F.


February 13th.                  Clear.  Later Rain.                  East Wind.

Direction: South.  Day's run 172 miles.
    Latitude        N. 23' 20' 33".
    Longitude       W. 159° 50' 45".
    Temperature 73° F.


February 14th.                  Clear.  Later Rain.                  East Wind.

From last night it has been clear and on the left we could see the Sandwich Islands.  After sailing for more than twenty days we were glad to see the mountains again.  Although it was dark we climbed up to the bridge to see land.  As we sailed along we passed two or three small islands.  We signalled to the pilot house and immediately a small boat came to guide us into the harbour.

As we had not shaved since we set sail more than 20 days ago we drew up sea water early in the morning and after shaving washed our hands and feet.  In the afternoon we arrived in the port of Honolulu on Oahu, the sixth island to which we came.  The harbour faces south and on both sides of it there are short sea walls.  Until we came into the harbour we did not see any houses on the water front.  On account of the clouds and thick mists we could not see the tops of the mountains.  Because of the tropical climate mists and clouds are frequent, The weather changes several times a day. The Sandwich Islands are in the North Pacific, scattered between N. 19° 50′ W. 155° 30′ and N. 22° W. 158°. This country is independent and consists of thirteen islands. The king's palace is on Oahu island. We anchored in port. The American minister living in Honolulu sent fruit to the head of our commission. This fruit which is called banana is like a fruit which we have in Japan and tastes like a makuwa melon. It is beneficial in cases of palsy, it is said. We landed at 2:00 P.M. At this time our ship fired a a salute. When we landed several conveyances came to meet us. These conveyances have four wheels and being drawn by two horses go very fast. By the side of the horses' eyes there are blinkers, three inches square, made of paper. They are used to prevent the horses from seeing to the right and left, it is said. After riding about three quarters of a mile we arrived at the hotel. On both sides of the street leading from the seashore to the hotel the natives were lined up to see us.

This hotel has five buildings. Of these our commission occupied three. In the main entrance of the hotel there is a bar. The back rooms on the second floor were reserved for the head of our commission. After rooms were assigned to us according to rank the hotel proprietor sent up fruit. This fruit consisted of water melon, musk melon, banana etc. The proprietor looked to be about forty years old. This hotel is not built of wood but of stone and tile. The walls are more than a foot and one half thick and look like a large Japanese store house. Because of the tropical climate the hotel is built in several separate units in order to avoid the heat. In front of the hotel there is a garden in which many beautiful flowers are blooming among which is cock comb. Although it is February the natives wear spring clothes on account of the mild climate. In Honolulu we saw the following vegetables which are native to certain parts of Japan also : kidney bean, lettuce, burdock, squash, corn, Irish potatoes etc. There are various plants and trees but there is no cherry, plum, pine, cypress, and bamboo.

The people of this island have a black and yellow skin, with eyes large and keen. The lower class people walk about bare-footed and they resemble painted demons. The higher class men wear shoes and clothes with tight fitting sleeves and trousers.

The higher class women wear a piece of white cloth wrapped around them reaching from the waist to the ankle. This material resembles Chinese cotton print. A white cloth is wrapped around their breast. They wear a white cloth thrown over their shoulders reaching to their waist like a shawl. The ladies arrange their coiffure around a comb which is about six inches long, shaped like a half moon. They wear a garland of flowers around their heads. Around their necks they wear a string of beads made of red berries. This seemed so strange to us. It is said that from birth they are simple but honest. Many men and women riding horses pass along the street. The pedlars carry their wares in a gourd some two feet in diameter thrown over their shoulder. The cost of living is very high. The price of a bath ticket is 2.5 sen (Note : 2 sen equal 1 cent). The hotel rates are one dollar per day for room and meals. Rice costs 16 2/3 cents per pound. Two bundles of charcoal cost one dollar. A little less than a pint of "sake" (rice wine) costs one dollar. Eggs are fifty cents a dozen.

On this island there is a great deal of sand but very little stone. Although it rains frequently water does not stand in the streets. There are no large trees on the mountains, but on the seashore there are many large palm trees. For supper we ate grey mullet and rice. At night we were troubled very much by the mosquitoes. Day's run 151 miles.

> Latitude     N. 21° 19'.
> Longitude   W. 157° 52'.
> Temperature 70° F.

February 15th.     Clear—Rain—Unsettled.

The ship is at anchor in the harbour. The king of Hawaii sent to the chief of our commission a mullet two feet long in a container made from a gourd. It is said that one hundred years ago the natives of this island were cannibalistic. Thirty years ago many English and Americans came to these islands and built schools and other buildings and taught the people to read and write. One hundred years ago the first Englishmen came to these islands. It is said that the natives captured the captain of the vessel and ate him alive, but that the sailors made good their escape and after returning to England reported the affair to their Queen. She sent warships to these islands and they captured eight women and carried them to England. During three years the English taught these eight women morals and ethics. Afterwards they were returned to their native land. The boat which took them back returned to England with many native products. From this time the islanders ceased to be cannibalistic. After this people from many lands came to these islands so that this port became very prosperous, but more than half the houses are occupied by British and Americans.

In the afternoon we walked through the middle of the town on a sight-seeing tour. After we had walked about a half mile we saw a large house. There were many musical instruments in it. Several people were playing the Hawaiian guitar, violin and castanet. We stood outside and listened because it was most interesting. One westerner came and led us upstairs. There we saw several hundred men and women in a large room which was about 100 feet by 50 feet. In the room were two tables 21 feet by 9 feet. On each table there were four balls made of ivory. In each corner of the table and in the middle of the longer sides were holes. The players used a stick about six feet long with which they hit the balls and tried to drive them into the holes. The player who succeeded in getting the ball into the hole won. When the ball went into the hole a music box played automatically. This was a signal that the game had been won, so the players drank wine and became very merry.

We went upstairs and turned to the left, where we entered another long hall in which the light was very dim because of the scarcity of the lamps. In this part of the building were about forty bedrooms. We thought this very strange and upon inquiry found it a house of ill fame. After the evening entertainment many of the guests retired to these rooms for which they paid $ 1.50 each.

After we finished our sight-seeing tour we returned to our hotel. After returning to the hotel we took a bath for the first time since leaving Japan. The bath was shaped like an egg. The depth was about one foot and a half. There were four baths and one boiler. The water was heated in this boiler and then ladled into the tubs. The cold water was put in first after which hot water was poured in until the temperature suited the bather. As Westerners dislike very hot water they use water that is only tepid. Since Japan is not a hot country we do not bathe in such tepid water. In the bathroom there was a white stone shelf on which there was a comb and soap etc. About sundown a fish pedlar came to the hotel bringing a very large lobster about one foot long. It was like a Japanese spring lobster, which is delicious.

February 16th.              Clear. Rain.

The boat is in the harbour. The king presented the chief of our commission with five chickens and several mullets. The messenger who brought these gifts was a Hawaiian lieutenant. His story is as follows : Twenty years ago a Japanese vessel distressed in a storm put into this island. The ship was destroyed and all of the crew of 12 were killed save one survivor. The people of this island cared for him. After he recovered he went to America and we have not heard of him since. The lieutenant brought a letter which had been written by this sailor. The letter was opened and the following was written in it: Masakichi Tayama, Japan. The letter was thought to be important, hence it had been preserved.

Every day the weather changes several times and above the roofs of the city both morning and late afternoon there are several rainbows, sometimes five or six. After lunch five of us went sight seeing. We went out of the hotel and turning to the left went about 2/3 of a mile to the outskirts of the city, where on the left side of the road we saw a large cycad tree. This tree was more than 20 feet tall and the diameter was about sixty feet. We saw a centipede also more than one foot long. As these islands are in the tropics there are many poisonous insects here. The street forked ; taking the left we went about ½ mile. At the foot of the mountain there was a beautiful three-story house. The yard was lovely with many flowers in bloom. We took a narrow walk and went in to see the flowers. A lady about 22 or 23 opened the glass door and came out. We bowed to her. She gave each of us a beautiful flower. She spoke a great deal to us, though we could not understand anything she said. Because the house was very fine we wanted to see it but the lady stopped us by gestures and seemed much worried. We thought that her husband must be absent and that she would be embarrassed if we went in, and bowing to her we withdrew from the garden. After going about a third of a mile we came to a cross road and taking the left we found a river flowing by the road. There were five or six native women taking a bath. Near by there were many taro growing in the water. Besides these there were no paddy fields.

After walking about ½ mile we came to the house of an American. As we were passing by the gate a lady about seventeen years of age called us in. We opened the gate and when we were going in a man about forty, who seemed to be the head of the house came out to meet us and led us into the house. There was a carpet on the floor and a large mirror opposite the door. Near the mirror there was a picture so that this was a very beautiful room. When we sat down we were offered candy and fruit.

Having stayed a little while we left this house and went about ¼ mile were we saw a large house. We went in and found it to be a bar. The bartender offered us a red drink which was bitter. Then he played the music box for us. He brought out a box about five inches wide and about two feet long, to both ends of which were attached short wires on the loose ends of which were jointed handles about three inches long. Two of us took hold of one handle each, then joined hands with a third person. The bartender turned a thing which looked like a nail and the three of us were shocked so that we shook from our heads to our feet. We could not move our tongues, nor could we release each other's hands so that we just looked at one another. When the bartender turned the switch we became free and learned that this was an electric machine. When we knew this we laughed and returned to our hotel.

As we walked along the street we saw a horse and cow. The cow's horns were more than two feel long; the horse's ears were about one foot long. In Japanese he would be called a rabbit-eared horse. They were grazing in a field. A whaling boat received permission today to sail from this port and is going to Hakodate.

February 17th.          Cloudy.          Windy.

We stayed in the hotel. A committee from our commission

called at the home of the minister about noon. In the afternoon we went for a walk in the town. As we were Japanese we attracted much attention. One person came out of the crowd and taking me by the hand guided us about a third of a mile to his house. We went into the house and saw a mirror, pictures, a clock and chairs in a beautiful room. We were served cake and white wine. The lady of the house was cleaning the parlor. After she finished she led us in and showed us many interesting curios, but as we had already stayed a long time we took our leave. We were informed that this was the home of a Britisher.

We then went to a large store to buy cloth to make kimono. The proprietor, a man about fifty years of age, came out and talked with us, but we could not understand him. He took us by the hand and led us into several rooms. This house is twice as elegant as the house which we just saw. The owner then led us up to a tower on the roof of the house. It was very high so that it commanded a view on all four sides from the mountain to the sea where the waves broke on the shore making an indescribably beautiful scene.

Down stairs an artist about thirty years of age made sketches of us. He was very accurate, showing in detail even our swords. When we complimented him on his drawing he was much pleased. The owner of this shop told us that this artist was well known among the British and Americans. And he also explained that the implement with which he did the drawing was made of gold and was called a pen.

About $\frac{1}{4}$ of a mile from this shop was a school, built of stone and tile, and surrounded by spacious grounds. There were several hundred children between seven and sixteen who studied reading and writing here. At sundown we returned to the hotel.


February 18th.                    Cloudy.

The chief of our commission called upon the King. The sailors from the American battleship carrying rifles marching to the music of the naval band and eight Hawaiian lieutenants in full dress riding on horseback escorted us. The Hawaiian lieutenants were dressed in uniform made of black woolen cloth embroidered with gold braid. Their head dress was decorated with three red feathers. The sword hangs from the left hip supported by a leather strap two inches wide. This is kept in place by a belt made of the small material. They wear this dress on military campaigns also.

We arrived at the king's castle, which is near the sea at the foot of the mountains. Many cannon were on the mountain behind the castle. Before entering the castle gate we alighted from our carriages. About forty soldiers carrying rifles and twenty officers carrying swords stood at attention as we came up. After we were shown into the audience hall the king came in to welcome us. Then the queen escorted by some twenty ladies-in-waiting came in also. The name of the king is Alexander and that of the queen is Emma. Although they live in a castle it is in reality a beautiful residence. The officers sheathed their swords and escorted the ladies to their seats.

As we returned to our hotel about two o'clock there were crowds of people lining both sides of the street. In the evening all the shops closed, and the people held a festival in honor of the safe arrival of the Japanese, it was said. There was much dancing to the accompaniment of the flute, drum, and Hawaiian guitar. They call this noisy sound music. At first there was only one man and one woman, but afterwards there were two men and one woman. The music was monotonous as there was no variety. The king and queen came to the festival and danced. When we saw this we realized that the rulers were familiar with their subjects.


February 19th.                    Cloudy.

Since we landed the king has sent fish to us each day. The fish are mullet. We have seen no other kind. Wild animals and birds are scarce on this island. We have seen chickens and pigeons only, but no small wild birds. One sees cows, horses, and dogs, but no wild animals in the woods.

About two o'clock we left the hotel and arrived at the boat about two-thirty. The ship which was so badly battered during the storm of January 23rd is undergoing repairs hence we are not yet able to set sail. A square-shaped boat is dredging the harbour so that large ships may dock. The machinery in the dredge is operated by steam power. The natives use a boat fifteen feet long by one foot wide which is hewn out of a tree.

Some 160 miles south of Honolulu there is the island of Hawaii on which is a very tall mountain. Throughout all four seasons this mountain is covered with ice and snow although it is in the tropics. Nearby there is another mountain which is a volcano from which smoke continually pours. This volcano is the highest mountain on these eleven islands.

On the seashore near the harbour of Honolulu there are grass huts built on platforms supported by wooden piles to raise them above high tide. As these houses seemed unusual I asked about them and was told that fifty years ago all the native houses were like this.

February 20th.                    Cloudy.

We left the hotel and went aboard the ship but remained in the harbour. About seven or eight hundred houses can be seen in the city from the boat. The length of this island is about sixty miles.

Temperature 75° F.

February 21st.                    Clear.

We are still in the harbour of Honolulu. Soon after 12 o'clock the head of our commission called on the American minister. He returned about four o'clock.

February 22nd.                    Cloudy.

The ship rides at anchor. We saw three or four ships far out at sea. They are whaling ships, it was said.

Temperature 76° F.

February 23rd.                    Cloudy.

The ship remained in the harbour.

Temperature 72° F.

February 24th.                  Cloudy.                  Rain in Evening.

The ship remained in the harbour.
Temperature 72° F.

February 25th.                  Clear.                  Shower.

The ship remained in the harbour.
Temperature 74° F.

February 26th.                  Cloudy.

The ship remained in the harbour. The king and queen paid a visit to the ship. After they inspected the ship, a salute was fired in their honour. They were then shown into the salon where they were served refreshments. The king gave a present of $70.00 to the sailors.

Sometimes when the ladies of this island go for a walk with their gentlemen friends they take their escort by the arm.

February 27th.                  Cloudy.                  East Wind.

About 2:00 P.M. our ship set sail in a southeastern direction.

February 28th.                  Clear.                  Northeast Wind.

Our direction has been changed to northeast. This morning we cannot see the Sandwich Islands—only a broad expanse of sea is visible. The ship is rolling and pitching so that it is quite disagreeable. But this storm is much less severe than the storm we encountered soon after leaving Japan. We spent the day in playing chess. Day's run 100 miles.

Latitude      N. 21° 58' 45".
Longitude     W. 156° 30' 30".
Temperature 74½° F.

February 29th.                  Clear.                  Northeast Wind.

Day's run 128 miles.
Latitude      N. 22° 59' 11".
Longitude     W. 154° 30' 55".
Temperature 73° F.

March 1st.                    Clear.              Northeast Wind.

Day's run 146 miles.
Latitude       N. 24° 43′ 43″.
Longitude     W. 152° 42° 15″.
Temperature 71° F.


March 2nd.                    Clear.              Northeast Wind.

Day's run 166 miles.
Latitude       N. 26° 37′ 14″.
Longitude     W. 150° 24′ 45″
Temperature 69½° F.


March 3rd.          Clear. Rain in Afternoon.    Northeast Wind.

On shipboard there was a sham battle instead of regular drill today. The sailors fired the cannon and rifles and used their bayonets and swords. The officers with drawn swords went here and there giving commands. Signals were given by whistle, drum and bells.

Day's run 210 miles.
Latitude       N. 28° 14′ 11″.
Longitude     W. 147° 10′ 30″.
Temperature 66° F.


March 4th.                    Cloudy.            Northwest Wind.

Day's run 230 miles.
Latitude       N. 29° 57′ 2″.
Longitude     W. 143° 18′ 20″.
Temperature 61° F.


March 5th.                    Clear.             Northwest Wind.

Day's run 248 miles.
Latitude       N. 31° 41′ 20″.
Longitude     W. 139° 2′.
Temperature 59° F.

March 6th.                    Clear.  Rain at night.           South  Wind.

> Day's run  221  miles.
> Latitude        N.  33°  16′  33″.
> Longitude      W.  135°  3′  45″.

March 7th.                        Clear.              Southwest  Wind.

Wind  very  favorable.   Ship  sailed  fast.

> Day's run  263  miles.
> Latitude        N.  34°  2′.
> Longitude      W.  130°  6′  5″.
> Temperature 63°  F.

March 8th.                  Clear.  Rain.

About  3:00  A.M.  a  light  was  sighted  on  the  northern  horizon.
It  was  reflected  on  the  surface  of  the  water  about  2/3  of  a  mile
away  and  glowed  like  a  red  sunset.   We  were  surprised  and  went
up  on  deck  to  see  what  it  was.   This  light  sometimes  appears  in
the  northern  ocean.    In  America  this  is  called  the  northern  light.
It  is  caused  by  vapor  from  the  evaporation  of  snow.   We  saw  this
light  clearly  through  a  telescope.    At  times  the  light  resembled
lightning.

About  4:00  P.M.  far  off  on  the  left  a  mountain  was  sighted.
This  is  a  small  island  in  the  possession  of  the  United  States  but  we
do  not  know  the  name  of  it.    About  10:00  P.M.  far  away  we  saw
a  lighthouse  near  San  Francisco.

> Day's run  270  miles.
> Latitude        N.  36°  57′  19″.
> Longitude      W.  125°  26′  15″.
> Temperature 60°  F.

March 9th.                  Rain.  Clear.

At  2:30  A.M.  our  ship  fired  a  shot  to  warn  another  ship
which  we  passed,  that  ours  was  a  warship.   Soon  after  six  o'clock
we  sighted  the  entrance  to  the  harbour  of  San  Francisco  in
California,  so  our  warship  ran  up  a  flag.   About  6:30  a  small  boat
came  to  pilot  us  into  the  harbour.   The  charge  for  this  service

was sixty dollars, it was said. At eight o'clock we passed through the entrance into the harbour. On each side of the entrance there is a small mountain with a lookout tower. The width of this entrance is about 2½ miles. About 2/3 of a mile from the entrance on the right is a lighthouse. To the rear of the lighthouse is a fort which is about 540 feet wide. It is built in three terraces the total height of which is about 90 feet; on each terrace there are many cannon. A bridge joins the rear of the fort to the mountain. After sailing about 2½ miles we arrived at the port of San Francisco. San Francisco Bay is very large but there are many small islands in it. On an island near the wharves there is a fortress. In the harbour many large ships were at anchor. When we arrived at the harbour our ship fired a salute. Among the ships was a Russian warship. The American warship on which we were travelling ran up a Japanese flag. The Russian vessel also ran up a Japanese flag and fired a salute.

California was Mexican territory, but now it is American territory. In all of America the richest gold mines are found near San Francisco. The gold comes from Upper California. Gold was discovered in 1840. At first about 5,000 men rushed into the gold fields. By 1850 the population had increased to 20,000. Many houses were built in Chinese style. But because of the frequent fires the houses were not built of wood but of stone which was plastered. The roofs are flat and are made fire-proof. At the present time, that is 1860, there are about 10,000. In 1805 the tax on gold mines was 250 gulden every four months, but in 1860 it is 25,000 gulden per month.

As San Francisco is very hilly, the streets are steep. From East to West there are 46 streets. From North to South there are 25 streets. Having stayed in the harbour a little while we sailed to the Navy Yard on the main land. We sailed up the river about 30 miles. The width of this river varied from one-half to a mile in width. On both sides of the river there are small hills on which the grass and trees are closely cut so that it does not seem pretty to us. The distant view from the ship is very fine, for the snow is still on the mountains. There are no large trees on either side of the river but the green grass covers the hills like a lawn. As there are very few houses it is quiet along the river bank.

When we arrived at the Navy Yard a ship at anchor there fired a salute. Our ship ought to have replied to the salute but as her guns were injured during the storm at sea and were being repaired she did not. Though the river is narrow at this point, yet it is so deep that even large ships can come alongside the wharf. The wharf is built of stone. The name of this river is the Sacramento. Above the Navy Yard this river is very broad so that it seems like the sea. The commandant and the officers live in six or seven houses at the Navy Yard. The Navy Yard is the place for building warships and keeping them in repair. On the opposite side of the river from the Navy Yard there are about 300 houses which resemble those we saw in the Sandwich Islands. They are built of brick and are three stories high. The people of the Navy Yard, not having heard from this ship since she set out to go to Japan to meet our commission, were relieved to see us. The Commandant of the Navy Yard sent us salmon and a shark which had been caught in the Sacramento river.

Day's run 150 miles.
Latitude     N. 37° 47'.
Longitued    W. 122° 22'.
Temperature 60° F.

March 10th.          Rain. Afterwards Clear.

At ten o'clock we went ashore and proceeded to the home of the commandant. On both sides of the gate are lanterns made of glass. The commandant's house is of three story construction and is quite pretty. Many beautiful flowers are blooming in the front yard. All Americans prize flowers and like them very much. We went to call on Lord Kimura, the head of our Commission, who was lodging at the hotel. About four o'clock we returned to our ship. In the evening we went ashore again in order to take a bath.

March 11th.          Rain.

Before noon we boarded a small launch and went down the river to San Francisco. Although this trip was beautiful as, I described the scenery before, I shall not do so again. We arrived about 2 P.M. In the San Francisco harbour there are more than ten wharves about 180 ft. long built of wood which look to us like wooden bridges. These are used for unloading the boats. As the sea is very deep here even large ships can come along the wharves. Many carriages came to meet us and we got into them. These carriages had glass on all four sides and were decorated with gold and silver colored finishings. On both sides of the front of the inclosed part of the carriages were square lanterns made of glass. These carriages accommodating four passengers were drawn by two horses which travelled very fast. A great crowd of people like a cloud lined both sides of the street from the wharf to the hotel to see us pass. So great was the crowd that we should have been unable to walk, but we managed to get through in the carriages. The five story hotel where we stayed was a large building. The hotel was called the Matheson International(?). We went into the hotel and were shown several rooms in each of which was a clock, looking-glass, fire place, and pictures hung on the walls. It was all so fine that our eyes popped out with amazement. There are more than 200 rooms in this hotel. In a corner of each room there is a cord which rings a bell in the office of the manager when pulled by a guest who wants any service. There is also a device near the bell which records the room number so that a bell boy may answer the call. This cord is made of wire. The device is a call bell. The hotel is so large that if the guest claps his hands for service as is customary in Japan he may not be heard, hence this convenient device.

When it was time for the evening meal a bell like a fire bell was rung and all the guests gathered in the dining room on the first floor. The size of the dining room was about 200 feet by 100 feet. There were long tables where men and women came and sat down in chairs and ate their meals together. We also went into this large dining room and ate western food. The first course served in large white bowls consisted of chicken soup in which there were very small dried fish. This soup was not savory. Sliced bread like small pieces of wood were served piled up on a large dish. Then a whole baked chicken was served. Rice was served in a large dish. This rice was grown in South America and though the color was white it tasted like Japanese upland rice and was not very good. The next course consisted of corn beef and cabbage served with white beans. Then sponge cake and sauce were served twice. Then boiled salmon and flat fish were served. Instead of tea, coffee was served. This coffee is so bitter that unless sugar is put in it one cannot drink it. Crackers were served with the coffee. Each person was served a glass of water. Vinegar, mustard, sugar, salt, and pepper were placed at intervals on the tables. It was said that this meal was a banquet and took a long time to prepare, but as it was not savory, being very greasy, we did not enjoy it, but because we were very hungry we ate a little of each dish. In each room there was a bed nine feet long. There were different kinds of single and double beds and over each there were mosquito nets which were like ours at home. As there were no mosquitoes they were used to keep other people from seeing the occupants. The beds were always left in the rooms. Every morning and evening the maids made up the beds. The length of the pillows was more than one foot. They were white. One of my friends who could not find his pillow though he searched the room, found a clean white jar under the bed which he used as a pillow and was happy. As it was hard he slept very well. In the morning when the servant saw this she was very much surprised. When we asked the reason for her surprise she said that as the hotel was very large and the toilets far from the bed rooms one of these jars was put in each room for the convenience of the guests. When we heard this, we all laughed.

In the evening many merchants came to the hotel and sold various articles to the guests. In this country the men greet the women by kissing their hands, and sometimes they greet by kissing each other.

When our chief commissioner boarded a launch at the Navy Yard the guns of the fortress fired a salute. The ship on which we arrived from Japan should have fired a salute but only fired one salvo. We thought this unusual and went up on the deck of the launch and looked over towards the "Powhatan." An officer had ordered the salute. It happened that the Commandant of the Navy Yard was walking on the river bank nearby so that the force of the explosion wounded him in the face, tearing his clothing and causing him to bleed freely and fall on the spot where he was talking at the time. Many people being surprised rushed out and took him home. This was the reason why the full salute was not fired.

March 12th.                         Rain.

We should have returned from San Francisco to our ship at the Navy Yard, but our chief Commissioner had to call on the city officials, so that more than half of our party who had no business in the city returned. Two or three of us went out of the hotel in a northeastern direction and on the way to the ship went on a sight seeing tour. After a short time we came to several large stores and then we saw three blocks of Chinese shops. In this Chinese quarter we saw the shop names and names of articles and drugs written in Japanese characters so that it made us feel very much at home. This seemed to us to be the most interesting part of the city. The Chinese women used red powder. We went up to a high place on the street and saw an excellent view. A man about thirty years of age came out of a house and invited us in. He insisted that we go in. When we did so he seemed delighted. He introduced his little boy who was about ten years old. He kindly brought out many interesting articles for us to see. But as it was time for us to go back to the ship we reluctantly took our leave and departed. In the autumn of last year he had come from Holland and settled here.

In San Francisco we saw large dogs over three feet high which were very fat. About eleven o'clock we took a carriage and went to the launch. About 3 o'clock in the afternoon we arrived at the Navy Yard. In the evening we went to take a bath in the Japanese ship " Kanrin Maru " which was tied up at the Navy Yard. We received pears and apples from a man aboard the " Kanrin Maru " but they were not very good.

At the Navy Yard as there was no well water, rain water was used for cooking. At midnight a large rat came into our room and we killed him. A sailor came in and taking the rat gave it to a small dog which ate it. This seemed strange to us.

March 13th.                         Cloudy.

We remained at the Navy Yard during the day and nothing especial happened until about seven o'clock in the evening, when the chief Commissioner returned to the Navy Yard from San Francisco. He told us his experiences in the city. He related how he went to the city hall which was as large as a theater in Japan. At each end of the hall was a balcony and a large platform was in the center. Certain officers from England, France, America, Russia, Holland and other countries and business men of the city were seated in the spacious hall in order of rank. As this was the first time the Japanese had come to San Francisco the American officer went up on the platform and after making a bow addressed the assembly in a loud voice. The Japanese Commission understood the bow, but not one word of the speech. After the welcome address was concluded there was a salute, followed by a banquet accompanied by music. On the way to and from the city hall he saw tapestries which the citizens had hung from their third and fourth story windows in honour of the occasion.

March 14th.        Cloudy.    Afterwards Fair.

After twelve o'clock we left the boat and went to the Navy Yard. This place is in the same latitude as Japan and as it is in the midst of spring the flowers of the fields are blooming and the scenery is beautiful. As the spring weather is very pleasant we went to gather plants, and while the sun was setting over the western hills we returned to the "Powhatan."

All articles are very expensive in this place. Three and one half pounds of rice cost one dollar. One salmon costs one dollar and a half. Eggs are one dollar per dozen.

Knowing that the Japanese are fond of bean curd the Chinese who live at the Navy Yard made it and sold us one large slice uncooked or ten small pieces fried for one dollar.

One of our officers went to call on the Commandant of the Navy Yard who was accidentally hurt a few days ago. Though he was painfully wounded, when he heard that a Japanese had called he got out of bed and came to greet him. While he wiped the blood from his face they conversed on various topics. The commandant in explaining the campaign of the Mexican War said that he lost one eye at that time. The burned powder got into his good eye and one side of his body had lost all feeling as a result of the accident the other day. He said it would be too bad to be blind, but that as he was over sixty it did not matter if he died. During the conversation he did not show any signs of weakness so that my friend said to him that he appeared very energetic.

March 15th.    Cloudy.    Strong Wind in Evening.

We stayed at the Navy Yard.    Yesterday five or six of our company went across the river to a town to shop, but as there was no boat and no bridge they were unable to return.    They waited in a saloon near the river landing, but as no boat came to meet them they became worried.    They made signs to the saloon keeper that they wanted to go back, so he took a Japanese flag and going down to the landing signalled to the " Powhatan."    As a small boat went to meet them they were relieved.    Today also some of our company went over to the town across the river and as there were no bridges or boats by which to return they hired a boat for one dollar and a half.

In the afternoon about two o'clock the captain of the " Powhatan " ordered her to sail from San Francisco for Washington. The band played and a salute was fired.    The officers wearing swords lined up on deck and the sailors climbed the rigging and called " good-bye " three times.    This is their custom when bidding farewell.

March 16th.        Cloudy.    Clear in afternoon.

There was a fire in San Francisco this morning.    The fire bell was rung and firemen gathered at the fire.    The only apparatus were hand pumps.    These pumps are kept in the quarters of the night watchman.    When a fire breaks out they are put on a hand cart and rush to the scene of the fire.    We were surprised to observe that all present were firemen with no spectators among them.    The people who lived next door took no interest in the fire and did not take their possessions out of their houses.    The reason why they were not worried was that the houses were ordinarily built of stone or brick instead of wood, hence only one house burned at a time.

A man of our company who had been employed by a large store in Tokyo went shopping and quarrelled and fought with two westerners.

March 17th.                          Cloudy.

We spent last night at the Navy Yard.   One of our servants became sick and remained in San Francisco.  We suppose that he returned home on a Japanese warship.   The servant who got in a fight yesterday was examined on shipboard and put in hand-cuffs.

Two or three Japanese who went shopping in San Francisco visited the theater.   The person who took the female role was a real woman.   In all other respects the play was just like Japanese plays, with love scenes and fighting, but as they did not understand the language they did not get the meaning of the play, but they followed the action of the play.   They went to a Chinese theater also where femine roles were played by men and though they did not understand the language they enjoyed the play because it was like a Japanese play.   Next to the Chinese theater there was a side show in which there was a man more than 8 feet tall.

Two or three of our company went across the river from the Navy Yard.   They hired a boat to bring them back and although the distance was only about 1/5 of a mile the price was three dollars.   If they used a little larger boat the charge would have been ten dollars.   We wondered why it was so expensive.


March 18th.

While the " Powhatan " was tied up at the Navy Yard many small boats came up to her, bearing merchants who came to sell their wares.   The people who lived on the land and those who were on the boats were forbidden to throw refuse into the river.

All ships which come from abroad and the small boats in the harbour have to pay a fee for the upkeep of the lighthouse and pier.   The lighthouse at the entrance to the Navy Yard can be seen for 25 miles down the river.

At four o'clock in the afternoon we raised anchor and sailed from the Navy Yard.   As we sailed out the Navy Yard fort fired a salute and our ship returned it.

This fort was built on a small island in front of the Navy Yard. The fortress consisted of a wall about nine feet high which was constructed of brick made from clay dug from a mountain on the island. There were 46 guns mounted on the wall. There was a lookout tower on top of the mountain.

March 19th.                    Clear.                    West Wind.

Day's run from 3/18/60 at 4:00 P.M. to 3/19/at noon 117 miles.
  Latitude      N. 35° 50′ 24″.
  Longitude    W. 122° 57′ 15″.
  Temperature 56° F.


March 20th.                    Clear.                    West Wind.

Direction : South—southeast. Favorable wind.
The boat made much speed. Day's run 250 miles.
  Latitude      N. 32° 10′ 4″.
  Longitude    W. 120° 42′.
  Temperature 63° F.


March 21st.                    Clear.                Northwest Wind.

Day's run 240 miles.
  Latitude      N. 28° 26′ 4″.
  Longitude    W. 119° 31′ 15″.
  Temperature 64° F.


March 22nd.                    Clear.                Northwest Wind.

About 8 o'clock this morning we saw a great school of salmon.
Day's run 210 miles.
  Latitude      N. 25° 6′.
  Longitude    W. 118° 25′ 15″.
  Temperature 65° F.


March 23rd.                    Clear.                Northwest Wind.

Direction : East by Southeast.
Day's run 211 miles.
  Latitude      N. 22° 40′ 39″.
  Longitude    W. 115° 34′ 0″.
  Temperature 72° F.

March 24th.                                          East Wind.

Day's run 202 miles.
    Latitude     N. 20° 49' 40".
    Longitude   W. 111° 35'.
    Temperature 74° F.


March 25th.          Clear.          Southwest Wind.

We saw three small islands on our right before four o'clock this morning. We are sailing east by southeast. The ocean is so calm that it looks like a great river. About two o'clock in the afternoon we saw a great school of fish about one mile from our ship. These fish are porpoise. They jump as high as six feet. Their backs are black and they are about four or five feet long and look like the bonito which live in Japanese waters. Just before dark a water fowl lit on the ship. The sailors called it a "bubo." It resembles the albatross which lives in the ocean near Japan. This bird disgorged a fish about six inches long. Today we put on our summer clothes. Day's run 216 miles.
    Latitude     N. 19° 7'.
    Longitude   W. 109° 15' 30".
    Temperature 82° F.


March 26th.          Clear.          Northwest Wind.

We saw a "bubo" again today. For the past two or three evenings the western sky has been very red.

Day's run 213 miles.
    Latitude     N. 17° 35' 12".
    Longitude   W. 105° 51' 15".
    Temperature 85° F.


March 27th.          Clear.          East Wind.

Direction : East by Southeast.

An instrument shaped like a sword was attached to the top of the foremast. A chain connecting with it ran down the mast and hung down overboard in the sea. This was done so that if lightning struck the ship it would drain off into the sea.
Day's run 204 miles.

Latitude      N. 16° 13' 15".
Longitude    W. 102° 38'.
Temperature 87° F.

March 28th.                Clear.               East Wind.

Again this morning we saw a great school of fish.
Day's run 230 miles.
Latitude      N. 14° 47' 15".
Longitude    W. 99° 4'.
Temperature 87½° F.

March 29th.                Clear.               East Wind.

About noon we saw a large turtle on the surface of the water.
His head was as large as a horse's head. We saw another school
of fish today. They gathered together because they had been
chased by larger fish, some one explained. During the evening we
saw in the northeast several flashes of lightning. It became severe
at night. As it was very sultry we could not sleep.
Day's run 215 miles.
Latitude      N. 13° 14' 47".
Longitude    W. 95° 36' 30".
Temperature 89° F.

March 30th.                Clear.               East Wind.

About seven o'clock this morning we were directly under the
sun. About noon it became cloudy and a cool wind sprang up so
that it felt refreshing. In the evening, again, there was much
lightning.
Day's run 215 miles.
Latitude      N. 11° 53' 47".
Longitude    W. 92° 15' 15".
Temperature 85° F.

April 1st.                 Clear.               East Wind.

On the water there was a flock of birds like sparrows. In the
early afternoon the steam engine got out of fix and the ship stopped
for about one hour in the great ocean.

Day's run 200 miles.

    Latitude     N. 11° 30′ 6″.

    Longitude   W. 89° 2′ 30″.

    Temperature 81° F.

April 2nd.              Clear.           East Wind.

In the evening it became cloudy. The night became as black as ink. There was a severe thunder storm.

Day's run 180 miles.

    Latitude     N. 9° 23′ 47″.

    Longitude   W. 86° 22′ 30″.

    Temperature 85° F.

April 3rd.       Half cloudy and half clear.     East Wind.

Direction: East by Southeast.

The mountains of Central America are visible. This is Mexican territory. From this time on we were always in sight of the mountains. About 2 P.M. we passed a British man-of-war going in the opposite direction. Both ships ran up their flags. An officer on each ship climbed up to the lookout and called greetings to one another by announcing the names of their respective ships and the name of the commander of each. Then they took off their caps and waved to each other three times.

Day's run 240 miles.

    Latitude     N. 7° 42′.

    Longitude   W. 82° 43′.

    Temperature 84° F.

April 4th.             Clear.           East Wind.

Direction: North by Northeast.

Since the day before yesterday we have been continually in sight of the mountains. The closest we have been to them has been about one mile. The sun is north of us. About 2 P.M. far off on the horizon we saw a foreign ship. Day's run 200 miles.

    Latitude     N. 7° 3′.

    Longitude   W. 80° 20′ 30″.

    Temperature 86° F.

April 5th.                Half Clear-Half Cloudy.            East Wind.

At 6:00 A.M. our ship arrived at a point about one mile from Panama harbour.   Since this habour is shallow large ships cannot enter.   At the entrance of the harbour there are several hundred small islands.   The scenery is indescribably beautiful.   We realized that these islands are inhabited when we saw two or three houses on one of them.   When our ship arrived the rising sun flag was displayed and a salute was fired.   Two British warships in the harbour returned the salute.   These warships were guarding the harbour.   As the harbour is an important shipping port and the scene of frequent trouble it is always guarded.   An American officer who is stationed in Panama came on board and a salute was fired. In the afternoon a sudden storm blew up accompanied by lightning and thunder.   As this region is in the tropical zone thunder storms are frequent all the year.

Pedlars brought fruit on board.   They brought bananas, oranges, pineapples, pomegranates, and a fruit which looks like a green peach, and melons.   All of them tasted very delicious.

After 2 P.M. our baggage was put into a launch.   In the evening many fire-flies flew around the boat.   We caught some of them and observed that they are the same as those which live in Japan.   Day's run 130 miles.

Latitude        N. 8° 17'.
Longitude     W. 79° 31'.
Temperature 95° F.

April 6th.                          Clear.                        East Wind.

At 7:00 o'clock in the morning a launch came for us and as we were getting into it the band struck up and a salute was fired by the ship.   The two other warships in the harbour replied to the salute.   After sailing about one mile in the launch we landed at the wharf which was about 1,000 feet long.   The wharf was constructed of wood and was roofed over.

About 9:00 A.M. we boarded a train that came to meet us. The length of each car was about 48 feet and the width about 12 feet.   Seats were placed on both sides of the car and there was an aisle in the center.   Twenty-eight persons could ride in one car.

There were eight cars joined together which were all drawn by another car which developed power by steam. Each car has four wheels made of iron. Eight years ago an American came here and built this at a cost of $4,000,000.00. They call these wagons steam cars. From Panama to Aspinwall (Colon) a distance of 57 miles the ticket costs $24.00. Forty soldiers carrying rifles came to guard us. Many sightseers came to the wharf to see.

The natives were brown and their hair very curly. They were naked and barefooted and their character was bad. If they could find any valuables in the baggage which they were carrying they would steal them and run away. Although the character of the natives worried the Americans they could do nothing to correct the conditions because this is Spanish territory.

The train was released and started. As it sped like an arrow we could not distinguish the trees and plants on either side of the road. The noise sounded like a thousand peals of thunder over one's head and no matter with how loud a voice one spoke he could not be understood. But the cars did not rock and they went very fast. A roadway was cut through the mountains and bridges built across the rivers so that it was level. Along the way the train stopped a little after eleven o'clock at a beautiful three story house built of brick and stone. This was a rest house. We ate lunch here. Lunch consisted of bread, raisins, a fruit like a peach, and beef. After travelling about another hour we reached Aspinwall. The distance of 57 miles between Panama and Aspinwall was covered in three hours. The reader will please consider this great speed! The natives of Aspinwall are the same as the natives of Panama. Some white people, chiefly Americans and British, also live here. The huts of the natives are very simple. Logs tied with vines form the walls, the roofs are made of palm leaves and the floor of rubbish. Even the horses and cattle are kept in better barns than these in Japan. People who come to this country from abroad have houses buit of brick and stone which are very fine. When we arrived a great crowd of people out of curiosity came to see us.

After sailing about a mile in a launch we boarded the American warship Roanoke which we learned had waited for us for more than a year. This ship is larger than the Powhatan, being 315 feet long and 51 feet wide. This warship has two tiers of cannon.

Those on top are of eight inch caliber and fire a shot weighing 60 pounds. Those below are of nine inch caliber and fire a shot weighing 80 pounds. There are 32 eight-inch cannon and 36 nine-inch cannon on the sides and there is one 10-inch cannon each at the bow and stern. The " Roanoke " was built in 1855. Her war complement is 550 men. But as she had come to Aspinwall simply to meet us and not for war she did not carry a full crew. There are five decks on this ship. As there are no cabins for the sailors they had curtained off a space on the second deck with canvass. They spread their blankets on the floor but had no worry on account of wind or rain. This was like camping out. As this is in the tropical zone we were worried on account of the climate but because we crossed over on the train we did not feel the heat. During the time it takes for a smoke business may be transacted by an electrical device between Panama and Aspinwall, a distance of 57 miles. This electrical device is made of wire but how it works I have not the faintest idea. Our baggage was transferred from Aspinwall to the " Roanoke " between four in the afternoon and night.

April 7th.                    Cloudy.                    East Wind.

After leaving Aspinwall harbour about 10:00 A.M. and sailing 20 miles we arrived at Porto Bello in Columbia after 12:00 o'clock. Long ago a Frenchman[sic] named Colombus sailing west discovered this country, hence it is called Colombia. At the foot of the mountains of Porto Bello there are springs of good water. The ships come here to fill their tanks with drinking water. A device called a pump is used by the sailors without great exertion to fill the tanks of the ship with fresh water.

Although this water comes out of a spring, yet it costs one cent a gallon. On both sides of this bay which is about a half mile wide there are high mountains. The only house here is like the houses in Panama in its simplicity. This is the temporary residence of an American who resides here to collect taxes on the water that is sold. This man is about 40, his wife about 30 years of age. They keep one servant who is a native. As there is only one house it is a very quiet place. There are 2,000 houses in Panama and the population is about 50,000.

April 8th.                    Clear.                    East wind.

We landed at Porto Bello at 10:00 A.M.   As we heard there were fine springs here we carried our soiled clothes so as to wash them.   But as this water is for drinking purposes only we could not wash our clothes.   We found a small pool of water but as the water was foul we could not wash our clothes, so we returned to the beach very much disappointed.   We undressed and went in the surf.   Those who could swim went far out into the deep water. The westerners on board the ship called to them to stop but as they did not understand what they said they went out farther.   The westerners called an interpreter and said that the deep water was poisonous.   When we came out of the surf we asked about the poisonous water, and were told that they said that in order to make us stop swimming, because if any accident should happen they would be greatly bothered.   While we were bathing we caught with our hands some small fish which were among the rocks.   As we found this very interesting we continued to search for fish.   We found what we thought was an eel about two feet long and were trying to catch it when a westerner coming up and seeing it was much surprised and said we should not catch it because it was a snake. When we heard this we came up out of the water one by one. We returned to the house and rested there a while.   The servant brought us a lizzard about two feet long which he had shot in the mountains.   This lizzard is an agama and its meat is delicious. Sometimes they grow to be 12 feet long and are very dangerous. In these mountains there are many strange birds and animals.   A native came in a boat bringing a large lobster which he wanted to sell for one dollar.

The sailors on board had a firing practice.   Their rifles were six feet long and their bayonets about one foot six or seven inches. They also carried swords which were used for jabbing but not for cutting.   They did not wear gloves or masks as do the Japanese when they fence.   They stood sideways as they practised.   They practised according to the commands of their officers.

We sailed from Porto Bello at 2 P.M.   When we had sailed about seven or eight miles we saw two large white rocks in the sea.   The ship sailed north.   About sundown a rainbow appeared on the right. We got some ice which was stored in the ship and put it into our drinking water. As the weather was hot it made the water better for drinking. This ice was stored in tubs in the hole of the ship. It had been secured from the high mountains near Boston in the U. S. A. There were two monkeys on board which were different from Japanese monkeys. Their arms and legs were long and their tails were more than two feet long. These monkeys could hang by their tails which they wrapped around a limb. Then they would swing their bodies back and forth two or three times and hurl themselves through the air to some object to which they would cling. The freedom with which these monkeys climbed was amazing. Their tales were like snakes. On the opposite side of the bay from where we landed was a small town of two hundred houses.

April 9th.                    Clear.  Cloudy.                    East Wind.

Last night two westerners were taken sick and died. One of them was a negro. This morning at eight o'clock the chaplain read the burial service. The bodies were wrapped in pieces of canvas and were weighed down with 50 or 60 lbs. of iron. It was said that the fish would not eat the bodies and because of the weights they would stand upright on the bottom of the sea. The ship rolled and pitched a great deal so that the sailors who were quartered on the deck were drenched by the waves.

Day's run 91 miles.
Latitude       N. 10° 58'.
Longitude     W. 78° 59'.
Temperature 84° F.

April 10th.                    Clear.                    East Wind.

Just after four o'clock we passed directly under the sun.
Day's run 119 miles.
Latitude       N. 13° 4'.
Longitude     W. 74° 32'.
Temperature 83° F.

April 11th.            Clear.            East Wind.

The westerners carved animals and birds out of ivory nuts. The meat of these nuts which are about the size of a ball is white and very hard so that it resembles ivory. They grow in the sea near Aspinwall, it is said. The brown palm nuts resemble Japanese persimmons in shape. The meat of these nuts is delicious. Out of the hull the westerners carved rings which resemble lacquer.

Day's run 137 miles.
Latitude      N. 15° 44'.
Longitude     W. 80° 10'.
Temperature 82° F.

April 12th.            Clear.            East Wind.

The sailors drill daily. Today there was an inspection but as it was similar to the inspection on the " Powhatan " I shall not describe it.

Day's run 183 miles.
Latitude      N. 18° 24'.
Longitude     W. 82° 34'.
Temperature 82½ F.

April 13th.            Clear.            Northeast Wind.

Direction : Northwest.

The sailors cast a net and caught some fish. They are dolphin. They are colored like a nightingale and were spotted pale green and yellow. They were about four feet long and were beautiful in appearance and delicious in taste. About 2 o'clock we sighted Cuba on the right. This island is Spanish territory and its population is about 1,207,000. The island is about 800 miles long. Its chief products are tobacco and coral. About 3 o'clock we sailed by Cape St. Antonio. There is a lighthouse on a rock in the sea less than a mile from the shore.

Day's run 123 miles.
Latitude      N. 21° 17'.
Longitude     W. 84° 29'.
Temperature 80° F.

**April 14th.**　　　　　　　**Clear.**　　　　　　**East Wind.**

We passed the island of Cuba on our right.　As we sailed by the island we saw smoke rising from a volcano.　This island is Spanish territory and though the United States is negotiating with Spain about the purchase of the island Spain will not sell.　When we consider these negotiations it seems that the foreign nations do not like war without sufficient reason.

Day's run 109 miles.

Latitude　　　N. 22° 57'.

Longitude　　W. 83° 44'.

Temperature 76° F.


**April 15th.**　　　　　　　**Clear.**　　　　　　**East Wind.**

The ship is sailing northeast.　About 3:00 P.M. on our left we sighted a mountain which is in Florida, U.S.A.　A ship is passing between us and the coast.　After 4:00 P.M. we passed out of sight of Florida.

About 10:00 A.M. an American steamship passed by about 250 yards away and the flags of both ships were dipped in salute.　It was a mail boat bound for Cuba.　The mail ship delivered newspapers to our ship.　These newspapers said that a certain incident had happened in Japan.　We were surprised that news of an incident which happened in Japan could travel 10,000 miles and be printed in a foreign country in a little more than 40 days.

About the same hour there was a roll call.　This was followed by a fire drill.　The westerners collected their belongings and hurried on deck.　About half of them brought fire-fighting apparatus and began to pump water from the sea into the ship.　This practice is intended to train them to put out a fire caused by a bomb thrown into the ship.

At sundown we sighted a sailing ship.　About 8:00 P.M. we saw a lighthouse some six or seven miles away on our left.　About 9:00 P.M. we sighted another lighthouse on our right about three miles away.　This was not on the island of Cuba but was on another, smaller island.

Day's run 170 miles.

Latitude　　　N. 24° 37'.

Longitude    W. 80° 48'.
Temperature 79° F.

April 16th.                Clear.            Northeast Wind.

The ship is sailing north. There are small islands on our right. During the afternoon we saw eleven ships.

Day's run 182 miles.
Latitude      N. 27° 24'.
Longitude    W. 79° 41'.
Temperature 79° F.

April 17th.                Clear.            Southwest Wind.

About midnight as the wind changed to the southwest the sails were set and the steam engines were stopped. In order to raise the paddle wheel out of the water, as the steam device was out of order, eight sailors got in the sea and pushed it up while several carpenters and sailors pulled it up by ropes. As the wind was very favorable we travelled fast and by nightfall were sailing in the open sea.

Day's run 223 miles.
Latitude      N. 31° 05'.
Longitude    W. 79° 04'.
Temperature 80° F.

April 18th.                Clear.            Southeast Wind.

In the afternoon the ship's equipment was examined and all that was not needed was left at the Navy Yard. Business can be transacted quickly over a cable which stretches from England to America. It is marvelous. This ocean is very stormy—so stormy that in one year more than one hundred vessels sailing between England and America are battered by the storm.

Day's run 146 miles.
Latitude      N. 33° 34'.
Longitude    W. 76° 42'.
Temperature 82° F.

April 19th.                    Clear.                    North Wind.

This morning we sighted two ships, one of which was a steam boat.  About 2:00 P.M. a dense fog settled over the sea so that it became as dark as night and we could not see.  The whistle was blown loudly at frequent intervals.  As this whistle was blown by steam the sound could be heard for a great distance.  After night fall not only was the fog horn blown but a gun was fired occasionally also.  Since the fog was so dense that it was impossible to see another boat coming or going the whistle was blown and the gun fired as is the custom on foreign vessels.

Day's run 173 miles.
Latitude      N. 36° 34′.
Longitude    W. 74° 30′.
Temperature 67° F.


April 20th.                    Cloudy.                    East Wind.

The ship is sailing north.  This morning we sighted four schooners.  We saw Barnegat Isle on the left at noon.  It is only a small island.  There is a tall lighthouse which is on a smaller island about a mile away.  During the afternoon we sighted several vessels.  About 2:00 P.M. a pilot came aboard from a small boat. This pilot came from New York and said the United States Government appropriated $30,000 to be used by the Port of New York to welcome the Japanese commission.  About 3:00 P.M. we sighted Shrewsbury.  We were now continually in sight of land as we were sailing about 2 miles off the coast.  About 4:00 P.M. we passed a steam boat and each boat dipped her flag in salute.  At 4:00 P.M· we arrived at Sandy Hook and anchored about a mile and a half off land.  About 40 ships were anchored in this harbour. We saw about 3,000 or 4,000 houses in the distance.  There were four lighthouses.  One of them was on a hill and appeared to be very high.  There are many houses on this mountain, it is said. Five officers who were messengers from the government came on board and said that we were to go to Washington instead of New York because New York had not yet made preparations to receive the Japanese.  It is said that it is fifteen miles from here to New York.  In the northeast about 2 miles away is Long Island.

Day's run 183 miles.
Latitude      N. 39° 21'.
Longitude    W. 74° 11'.
Temperature 61° F.


April 21st.                    Cloudy.                    East Wind.

The ship was anchored off Sandy Hook today.    We set sail for Washington but all the Americans are dissatisfied.  However, nothing can be done about it,    About 10:00 A.M. the commander went to New York to send a telegram to Washington saying that those aboard did not wish to go to Washington before New York. Until today it was not decided whether we should go to New York or Washington.   About 2:00 P.M. the Commandant of the Fort of New York came out to the "Roanoke" on a steamboat.    He had heard that the Japanese were bringing a newly invented gun ; hence he had come out to see it.   After inspecting the gun which he was very glad to see he returned.

In Japan papers are printed once or twice a month but in western countries they are printed daily although the news is only slightly different.   The fact that the Japanese have come to America is printed in several papers.   One newspaper says the Japanese are short of stature but are upright in character.    And that they are skillful with guns and swords and are very brave.   This is the first time they have been abroad but they are not afraid and go for walks in the city.   They are honest and do not steal.   The members of this commission are selected from among the "SAMURAI" who are the warriors of Japan.   They carry a Japanese sword which is a dangerous weapon.   This in outline is what the papers say about the Japanese.


April 22nd.                    Cloudy.                    Southeast Wind.

Last night the commander returned from New York at midnight.  He decided that we should sail for Washington.   At 11:00 A.M. we raised anchor and sailed from Sandy Hook.   We sailed southeast and were in sight of land on our right.   We sighted several ships.  Temperature 61½° F.

April 23rd.　　　Rain. Clear in aftrrnoon.　　Southeast Wind.

The boat is sailing south. The rain came in through the port-holes and caused us much inconvenience. One sailor became sick and died today. He was buried at sea. As I described a burial at sea some time ago I shall not repeat. After 4:00 P.M. we met an American warship and each ship fired a salute. The sailors climbed up the rigging of the masts and called " good-bye " three times to the sailors of the other ship. The meaning of " good-bye " is farewell, it is said. The name of that warship is " James-town." From sunset we sailed west. On the left we saw land. It is called Cape Henry. On it there is a tall lighthouse. About 6:00 P.M. we entered Hampton Roads and cast anchor about two miles from land. It is 240 miles from Sandy Hook to this place.

Day's run 188 miles.
Latitude　　　N. 37° 27´.
Longitude　　W. 74° 41´.
Temperature 59° F.


April 24th.　　　　Clear. Cloudy.　　　　East Wind.

In this harbour many large boats are at anchor and small boats are sailing about. The scenery is particularly lovely. As this is a bay the sea is calm. Since we shall land in Washington tomorrow we are very glad. At 10:00 a government steamboat came from Washington to convey us to the capital. The name of this boat is " Philadelphia." On the deck there was a band of sixteen musicians dressed in red uniforms. We boarded the " Philadelphia " about noon. There are four decks on this ship. The top deck is used as the lookout. We entered by the second deck and saw a beauti-ful flower carpet on the floor of the saloon, and mirrors and many pictures on the walls. There were several chairs in the room up-holstered in velvet. It was said that this furniture was especially made in our honor. In the next room there are forty double deck beds. There are sixteen other cabins with six beds each.

The steam engines are in the next deck below. Forward from the engine room is the store room. Aft from the engine room is the dining room. On both sides of the passage leading to the dining room are the kitchens, near which are the barber shops.

Our bedrooms are aft on the deck below the dining room. There is a beautiful carpet on the floor of our bedroom and even the passage leading to the toilet is decorated in gold and silver trimmings and is so fine that I cannot describe it.

At 2:00 P.M. the band played ; a salute was fired and we went in to lunch. It was a wonderful meal consisting of beefsteak, pork, chicken, rice, bread, and so forth. The wine was red, yellow, and purple and was of various taste being sweet, bitter, or flavored with peppermint. There was also sponge cake, oranges, apples, cake made of white sugar, milk, etc. Then there was a very unusual dessert. It was made of ice. It was of different colors and shapes and was very sweet. It melted quickly upon being put in the mouth and the taste was good. The name of this is ice cream. In order to make it, it is put in a vessel which is turned in hot water. Then it is put into a churn surrounded by ice. If eggs are not put into it at this time it will not freeze. Besides this there were several kinds of jelly all of which we ate but we did not know how they were made.

At 2:00 P.M. our ship sailed east and the officers and sailors of the " Roanoke " came on deck. There were several hundred sailors. Some of them climbed on the rigging of the masts and in a loud voice bade us farewell, and taking off their caps waved to us as the Japanese do when they are calling one to come to them but which is the American way of waving good-bye.

About 4:00 P.M. we anchored near a fortress. We landed and went to see it. This fortress was built of stone. There was a walk way on the wall. The wall surrounding the fortress was about one third of a mile square. In this wall there were many portholes about one yard square through which the cannon were fired. There were 468 cannon. Cannon balls pilled up on the ground looked like a mountain. Inside and outside the fortress there were about 100 houses. The officers and their wives lived in these houses. It seemed strange that the officers' wives should live in the fortress, hence I asked, and was told that when the officers went out to fight the wives prepared the food and sent it to their husbands, and if the husbands are killed the wives go and die with them ! Near the sea there is a tall watch tower. At night it is used as a lighthouse. Near the lighthouse there is a wooden pier about

700 feet long where freight is landed. There is a small warehouse nearby. Some forty soldiers armed with rifles guard the pier. It was here that we landed. There is a small island in front of the fortress separated from it about 700 feet. There are five houses and about thirty cannon on this island.

About 5:00 P.M. we left the fortress and sailed east. The officers, their wives, and soldiers called and waved good-bye. From 6:00 P.M. we sailed northwest. Temperature 63° F.

# DIARY OF VOYAGE

## Volume II

April 25th.                    Clear.                    Northeast Wind.

The ship sails west.    The river is about a quarter of a mile wide.    The water is dark.    The name of the river is the Potomac. We had a western meal this morning.    About 8:00 A.M. we cast anchor off the shore of Virginia.    There were only about five or six houses on the shore and a small pier.    We weighed anchor and after sailing about ten miles came to Mt. Vernon on our left.    The scenery here is very beautiful.    This is the place where the first President, George Washington, retired.    After the President died he was put in a glass coffin so that even now he looks like a living person.    The reason is that the coffin is air tight, it is said.    It is about 19 miles to Washington.    About one mile above Mt. Vernon on the opposite bank is a fortress.    The foundation of the fortress is built of stone and the wall of brick.    I do not know how many cannon are in this fortress.    About noon we arrived at the fortress of the Potomac Navy Yard in Washington.    Near the river bank there were about 1,000 soldiers drilling with rifles.    There was also a brass band.    There were about 100 mounted soldiers carrying sabers.    The soldiers' uniforms are gorgeous.    Many carriages were waiting for us.    For each of the three chief commissioners there was one carriage drawn by four horses.    The rest of us rode by twos, threes, and fours in carriages drawn by two horses.    As soon as we got in the carriages they formed in line.    Mounted soldiers followed by a brass band led the procession.    On both sides of the procession soldiers marched as our escort.    Two battalions of in- fantry and a brass band followed.    Several thousand people came to see the procession.    Some rode on horseback, some were in carriages, some had climbed up trees, others were sitting on walls or looking out of windows and the streets were packed with people standing. When the procession stopped en route the by-standers took their hats off and some of them came and shook hands and spoke to us.    A child about two or three years old was brought to us.    He shook hands and welcomed us and was very happy. A group of children between seven and eighteen rushed up to greet us. It was a lovely sight. A negro put his hand into the carriage, but none of us shook hands with him.

As the procession passed along old men and many women and children waved to us from the sidewalk. Many ladies waved white handkerchiefs, Japanese flags which they had specially made, or American flags from the windows of their houses on the second, third, fifth and sixth floors. After riding about two miles we arrived at the hotel. About 100 soldiers armed with rifles stood at the door of the hotel to guard us. A large Japanese flag was flying from the hotel roof. We got out of the carriages and entered the hotel according to rank. The soldiers who escorted us formed in two columns and to the accompaniment of the bands returned.

The hotel which is seven or eight stories high is built of brick, and does not have any posts in the rooms. It occupies one side of a city block and has two bars, a drug store, a barber shop, a cosmetics shop, tobacco shop, book store, etc., so that we were surprised at its great size. All the bedrooms had mirrors, clocks, pictures, beds, tables, chairs, bureaus, mantelpieces, fireplaces, carved statues, etc., which were wonderful. The papers reported that the Japanese arrived at noon. Hence a great crowd of sight-seers came to the city from distant places. As they travelled by railroad they could come one or two hundred miles or more in one day, which to them is the same as a journey of twenty miles in Japan. Even at sundown there was a great crowd of people gathered outside of the hotel. We threw Japanese iron coins of very little value from the second story window and the crowd scrambled for them.

The people of this country, both men and women, are white. The men wear clothes made of wool which are close fitting with various kinds of hats which I shall not describe. The officers' full dress consists of white trousers, dark coat with epaulet made of gold braid. Gold bands about one inch wide are worn on the sleeves. The officers of highest rank wear three gold bands. There is a gold band around their hats and in front an eagle or anchor worked in gold. They carry only one sword. When they go to war they do not use this uniform.

The women wear silk instead of wool. When they wear evening dress they do not wear a hat but part their hair in the middle so that both sides are alike and their arms and shoulders are bare. They use perfume and oil so that their hair is lusty and though the majority have light brown instead of black hair yet they are very pretty and look like a waxed doll. They wear a ring on their arms called a bracelet made of gold or coral inlaid with jewels. They cost between $100 and $1,500. In the bracelet they keep a little hair cut from their parents, brothers or sisters. Both men and women wear rings on their fingers. They resemble Japanese abacus balls. The ordinary dresses of the women have tight fitting sleeves with which shawls are worn over their shoulders. Their dresses are made differently from the clothes for men. From the hips down they wear a dress containing whale bone, the same material that is used to support a Japanese lantern. They are called hoop skirts. The diameter at the bottom is about three feet so that the feet are not seen. They sweep the ground. The girls eleven or twelve years old wear dresses down to their knees. Some of them have five or six tucks in their dresses which are quite pretty.

Poor people cannot wear silk dresses because they are expensive, but they wear printed cotton. But we did not see any one with torn or dirty clothes. We did not see even one beggar. The silk which the women wear cannot be made in America, so the raw silk is sent from China to France where it is woven into cloth and shipped to America. It is said that the styles of Europe and America come from France. The style of hoop skirts which look like Japanese lanterns came from France about four years ago. From today all of our meals will be foreign style hence, I shall not describe them.

At night there is a lantern made of glass in front of each house. Some houses have two or four so that the street is so well lighted that it is not necessary to carry a lantern—it is almost as bright as day. About seven o'clock we took a bath. The bath tub is 2½ feet wide, nine feet long and was lined with tin. There is a hot and a cold faucet. We were surprised at the flow of water. Two swinging doors opened into the bath. One guest at a time entered the bathroom, locked the doors from the inside, and bathed. One person bathed at a time so that others would not see the naked bather.  A flower carpet was spread on the floor of the bathroom up to the bath tub.  Near the bath tub was a looking-glass underneath which was a washstand with a marble top.  A comb, soap, and towels were on the washstand.

As the Japanese do not think it unusual to be seen naked, several of us bathed together.  The Americans were very much surprised to see this and went away.  After this none of them came to this part of the hotel when the Japanese went to the bath. There is a carpet on the floor of the toilet even.  The toilet is equipped with a device for flushing it.

We saw many unusual things but I shall not attempt to describe them, as I am not skillful enough.

April 26th.                    Clear.

Many carriages pass early in the morning.  We went to the bath again this morning.  At any time, even at midnight, hot water runs when the faucet is turned.  In the toilet also the hot water is on tap at all hours.  In the cellar there is a boiler from which the hot water flows to all parts of the hotel.

The laundry is not done by hand, but all the laundry is put into a large tub and turned so that it is washed better than when it is done by hand.  Instead of wringing out each piece separately the laundry is put in a large perforated circular container six feet in diameter which is revolved so rapidly that the water runs out.  Near the boiler there is a room twenty-four feet square in which the laundry is hung.  It is dried quickly by steam heat.  All of this equipment is so perfect that we were amazed.

Both outside and inside the hotel was crowded with people who had come to see us.  When we went into the hall they shook hands with us.  We could not help ourselves but had to shake hands with all who pressed upon us from all sides.  There were so many people trying to shake hands with us that we could scarcely press forward.  There were so many people that it was inconvenient to walk about in the hotel.  No one was allowed to enter the hotel without special permission, but the relatives of the government officials all had permits.  This is the Willard Hotel on Fourteenth Street, Washington, of which Mr. Frederick Brown is manager.

There are 800 rooms in this hotel. There is a bell cord in every room. When the guest wants service he pulls a bell cord which rings a bell downstairs and indicates the room. There are eighteen flights of steps with 175 steps from the first to the top floor.

Five or six ladies came and taking us by the hand, showed us the rooms of the hotel and the roof garden. We went up to the eighth floor, from which we could see in all four directions the beautiful scenery. It is about one hundred feet from the ground to the roof. The roof is made of iron plate about three inches thick covered over with white pebbles.

When the President of this country is to be elected four or five of the leading men of the government choose a candidate who is nominated by the party convention. This candidate then stands for election in the presidential campaign. Any one of good character except a negro may be elected president.

When the officials of the government go out on official occasions they wear full dress. When they are at home not on official duty they wear ordinary clothes and engage in business or farming. The President and members of the government sometimes go for a walk wearing ordinary clothes without any bodyguard, and no one recognizes them or speaks to them. When the President or other high officials go to a private house they remove their hats. It seems that the people think a great deal of their country but not half so much of their President. The people have to pay a tax to the government, but not a tax on land. In this city there is a place where the tax is collected from all over the country, and from this money the President and other officials are paid their salaries. The President is paid $40,000 or $60,000 each year. I have heard of both figures but do not know which is correct.

In this country when two people speak to each other as they pass on the street they take off their hats. When they meet they grasp each other by the hand and raise the hands and lower them three times. When a man meets a lady the most intimate greeting is to kiss her in the mouth. The next in intimacy is for the man to kiss the lady's hand. Then for the man to kiss his own fingers and throw the kiss to the lady.

In the evening when the gas lights are lit the hotel is as bright as day. The gas lights like Japanese hanging lights are made of silver or gold and are decorated with figures of birds, animals, grass, trees and flowers.   On one chandelier there are three, five, seven, or eight lights with glass shades.   A match is used to light the gas. The match is like the Japanese spill but is very different, for when it is struck it lights of its own accord.   When the lighted match is applied to the gas light fire flames up from it.   This is coal gas so that oil and wick are not needed.   This gas burns just as it comes out of the gas jet.   There is a valve which can be turned so as to increase or decrease the light.

April 27th.                              Clear.

Many sightseers came to the hotel this morning.   The three chief commissioners called on the Secretary of State at noon accompanied by an aide-de-camp each, leaving the hotel door in carriages.   They returned about one o'clock.   They said that the home of the Secretary of State was not as fine as the hotel.

In this country when a man and woman walk together they usually join arms.   It is very unusual for a woman to walk on the streets alone.   A young lady who is engaged walks on the street with the man to whom she is engaged.   In order to marry the man must be tweney-one and the woman eighteen.   They cannot drink according to law until they reach this age.   As they are not fully grown before this age, if they marry younger they will get sick, hence this law.   About 4:00 P.M. our baggage arrived at the hotel and was carried to the rooms.   A boy named Ray who had been on the steam launch with us came to the hotel and lifted a bottle of mercury which we bought in San Francisco weighing about eighty-two pounds.   We praised this boy for his unusual strength. The boy's sister also lifted this bottle easily.   The girl was sixteen ; her face was white and she had very pretty features.   It seemed very remarkable for her to be able to lift so heavy a weight.   She had four friends about 16 or 17 years old who each equally easily lifted this heavy bottle·   We were surprised to see these young girls lift an 82-pound weight.   We praised the boy for lifting the weight, hence the girls also did it.   Because we were so surprised the children returned home very glad.

In the evening there was a dance at the hotel.   This dance was accompanied by the piano. The sound of the piano resembles the Japanese koto but the shape of the piano is quite different. It is a large square shaped instrument. In the dance the man and woman take each other's hands and step from right to left but do not move their hands. When we saw this it looked to us just like exercise and did not seem a bit interesting. But we thought the clothes were pretty.

April 28th.                              Clear.

Many people gathered this morning. We are going to the home of the ruler in carriages this morning. We are putting on our finest kimono. Three aides-de-camp, two servants and one spear-bearer will accompany us. In front of the hotel on both sides of the street soldiers armed with rifles are lined up. A band composed of forty men in red uniforms led the procession. Sixteen cavalrymen armed with swords followed. There were about 1000 in the procession. Here and there among the crowd are photographers taking pictures of the procession.

When we arrived at the President's house we saw that it is surrounded by an iron fence with one large entrance but without any tower or pond in the yard. A captain meets us and guides the three chief commissioners. All of us wait in a room near the entrance. There is a flower carpet on the floor and many flowers arranged around the room. We walk along a hall about 180 feet until we come to double doors. Opening in this hall there is another room where the President is. The doors of the reception hall are opened and we go in. There is a raised dais on which the President and his wife sit. The ruler of this country is called President. He is President Buchanan. He is about sixty years old. His wife is about forty years old. Next to the President is the Secretary of State and other officials of the government. Several ladies are standing near the President's wife. They are dressed in ordinary clothes so that they seem quite comfortable. Only our chief commissioners went to pay their respects to the President while we waited in another room, but afterwards we passed by the reception room and saw it. There is no policeman in the President's house and no fortress in his yard. It is very beautiful but quite different from what we expected.

We returned to the hotel soon after one o'clock and were greeted by a crowd of people. Soon after two o'clock we went by carriage to call upon the Secretary of State, the Secretary of the Treasury, the Secretary of the Navy, the Postmaster-General, the Secretary of the Interior, and the British Minister, and we passed by the French and Dutch Legations.

In the evening when I went out in the hall of the hotel on business a man asked me for my card. And as I did not have a card I wrote my name for him. Then many other persons came up and asked me to sign my name for them, which I did, but as there were several hundred I stopped and returned to my room.

April 29th.                    Cloudy.

Many sightseers came to the hotel this morning. Each day we eat foreign food which is prepared by hand at a great cost of time. We have beef, pork, fried chicken, boiled chicken and other things which lack salt and are not savory. There is one dish which some of us cannot eat because of the odor, but others seem to enjoy it. Sauce, salt, vinegar, sugar, etc., are on the table.

About two o'clock we called at the Russian and British Legations. We took tea at the Russian Legation, but the British Minister was absent.

We opened our baggage and arranged in our rooms the presents brought from Japan for the President. We were asked by the Captain who acted as our guide for permission to take a picture of the presents. Among the presents were a sword, saddle, screen, pictures, book case, writing set, etc.

The three chief commissioners went to the home of the Secretary of State at 8:00 P.M. for dinner, after which they saw many beautiful women at a dance. It was a very cordial welcome.

April 30th.          Cloudy. Rain in afternoon.

Again many sightseers came to the hotel. The Americans were very kind to us. Each day members of the entertainment committee came to call, with a doctor to inquire after our health. Seven or eight soldiers guarded our rooms even at night. Each morning two chamber maids cleaned our rooms.

About 1:00 P.M. - there was a fire a block from the hotel. When the fire alarm was sounded the firemen rushed to the fire. One fire company with a wagon equipped with pumps and ladders extinguished the fire. With this pump they were able to throw much water on the fire. The buildings in the vicinity were all of brick and stone, so that the people were not worried that more than one house would burn. The occupants of the house escaped without attempting to rescue any of their furniture. Sometimes several persons die in a large building, it is said.

Two or three westerners brought guns and swords to the hotel and showed them to us. About 4:00 P.M. our chief commissioners went to a musical recital at the President's residence. There was nothing except music.

May 1st.                    Clear.

Again many sightseers came to the hotel. Because it is Sunday all the stores are closed. The people go to their temples to hear a sermon. The people of the whole country are Roman Catholics. There are temples here and there in the city. Men and women both gather to hear the sermon. In the intermission they sing and chant. The principal object of their worship is the image of a naked man about forty nailed through his hands and feet to a cross, and whose side is pierced.

The people of this country are not allowed to drink whiskey freely except on Sunday and Monday.

After one o'clock we went for an afternoon walk in the city but could not ramble freely about as we had to stay with our guides and guards. After walking about half a mile from the hotel we came to the President's house. There is a spacious lawn near his house and on the lawn an equestrian statue of the second President showing the horse rearing on its hind legs and the President carrying a drawn sword. The statue of the President is ten feet high. The statue is well proportioned and is made of bronze. The base of the statue made of granite is 12 feet high. An iron fence protects it. The citizens come here to rest and play. After walking about one quarter of a mile we came to another lawn where there was a statue of Washington, the founder of the United States. It is like the former statue. About ½ mile from Washington's statue there is a hill which is surrounded by a fence. There is a wide lawn within the enclosure and a rest house. This house commands a beautiful view of the river and the mountains. We rested here and after having a cold drink returned to the hotel about 3:00 P.M.

In the evening there was a concert at the hotel in a very large room which was about $120 \times 60$ feet. On the balcony above the entrance was a musical instrument. One musician could play it so that it sounded like a ten-piece orchestra. It was a very large instrument. Many chairs were arranged in the large room. The Japanese sat according to rank and were photographed. It was very troublesome to arrange for the picture but before we were aware it was taken without our knowledge.

May 2nd.                    Clear.

Leaving the hotel about 10:00 and walking about 2/3 of a mile we arrived at a large building. It was built by the government. Clothing, birds, animals, grass, trees, furniture, various unique articles, shoes, sandals, and agricultural implements from foreign countries are kept here. We noticed the model of a house, and ten models of a woman in the successive stages of pregnancy inclosed in a box with a glass top. There were so many exhibits that we were surprised but could not examine each in detail. This building is 360 feet square and is supported by posts here and there. It is built of granite. We returned to the hotel at noon.

In the evening there was a sudden storm when the wind blew, the sky became black, the rain fell and the lightning flashed. It soon passed away and cleared off.

May 3rd.

About eleven o'clock the chief commissioners called on the President to hand over the treaty regulating trade between Japan and the United States. They returned about one o'clock.

About 3 o'clock we called on the Dutch minister. There we

saw many beautiful ladies dancing and enjoying a banquet of beef, pork, chicken and cake which was served beautifully. The banquet table was decorated with many lovely flowers. The big cake was arranged on a large cake plate and was decorated with Dutch and Japanese flags. We returned to the hotel about five o'clock.

The President has two nieces the younger of whom, about 23 years of age, is famous throughout America for her beauty and intelligence. She acted as Secretary to the President and the government was carried on at her command, it is said. Neither of the nieces is married.

Ladies are highly honoured in America. When ladies are in a room and a guest enters he speaks to the ladies first and afterwards to the gentlemen. It is the custom for a man to remove his hat when he meets a lady, but not when he speaks to another man. When a gentleman meets a lady on the street he stands aside so as to let her pass first. In this country a lady is honoured as parents are in Japan.

When a person meets his near relatives he greets them with a kiss, and when he greets other relatives or a close friend he shakes hands warmly, but with others he simply clasps hands.

May 4th.                          Clear.

Again many sightseers came to the hotel.

The negroes have a bad disposition, though they are a simple folk. They are not rich. There is a gap between the white man and the negro and the white man has made the negro his slave. The negro is not allowed to go into the hotel, the auditorium, the tea house, theater etc., where the white man goes.

There was an entertainment given in the hotel in which dancers like Japanese geisha took part. They are called dancing girls. Some three hundred boys and girls from seven or eight to twenty-two or three years of age danced. The dresses of the dancing girls consisted of hoop skirts made, as I described before, of whale bone covered with light cloth, and a tight fitting bodice of heavy material trimmed with lighter material.

Some of the girls wore bonnets, some carried castanets, and at times they danced with the boys and at other times about 40 of them danced in a circle. In comparison with the Japanese dance their step was very fast. When the spectators wished to praise the dancers they clapped their hands and stamped their feet. The boys who danced wore ordinary clothes.

The ladies are very careful not to expose their breasts, so when they wish to nurse their children they do not withdraw their clothes from their breasts but they put the child's head inside their waist so that he may nurse.

May 5th.                              Clear.

About eleven o'clock the three chief commissioners went to the Capitol building. Then at noon they called on the Secretary of State. At 2:00 P.M. we went to the Navy Yard· At the Navy Yard instruments are made of gold and silver and copper and iron. Steam engines, cannon and other war equipment are manufactured here. In this arsenal most of the work is done by machinery rather than by hand, but I am not able to describe accurately this machinery.

The citizens of this city were very glad to see us and wished to welcome us, but as they were not allowed to enter the hotel, when we went on the streets they invited us to their homes where they entertained us with tea and wine. They invited the neighbours in to join in the fellowship and asked us for our visiting cards.

When we walked on the streets usually a crowd of people surrounded us and pressed upon us to shake hands. There were so many that three or four shook hands by each hand at a time, and when a person had shaken hands he did not come back a second time.

May 6th.                              Clear.

About 5:00 P.M. the chief commissioners went to the President's house for dinner. It was a splendid banquet.

The ladies' dresses are very beautiful, for they use expensive material. Even ladies carry a watch. The evening gowns of wives and daughters of very rich men cost from $1,000 to $10,000, hence poor men cannot marry. If a man does not have more than

$100,000 he cannot build a house. Building material is very expensive and there is a government law that small houses cannot be built, it is said. The people of Ameriea are big hearted, honest and faithful. The Americans do not scorn foreigners and are kind to strangers. The American people are simple and honest like Japanese born in the mountains or on the farm who have never been spoiled by the big city. The Russians are like the Americans. The English are jealous and have a very bad disposition. Occasionally they cheat others and are impolite. Because we came to America they are jealous, hence we are more carefully guarded. A cartoon printed in the newspaper showed a Japanese and an American walking hand in hand while an Englishman stood by looking on, gnashing his teeth.

May 7th.                         Clear.

We went for a walk after twelve o'clock. After walking about half a mile we arrived at a place which is like a temple. The grounds of this place are spacious and the building is large. We passed through the main entrance into the hall and went up to the second story. In the building was a lecture platform built up high above the floor. Before it were many seats. On the walls of the hall there were pictures portraying the sorrows and joys of life from birth to death.

By the side of the platform there was a recumbent statue carved in marble of a nude woman larger than life size. In an adjoining smaller room was a map of the world, and a concave mirror which enlarged our faces to four feet in diameter when we looked into it. In another room specimens of gold, silver, copper, and iron ore from different countries were on display. We went down to the first floor. There we saw many unique exhibits even more varied than we saw in the museum which we visited formerly. We saw a Japanese exhibit consisting of a spear, long sword, short sword; kimono worn at the court of the Shogun; kimono, skirt, and coat of the common people; various kinds of cloth; pieces of small furniture, sea shells and farming tools. Besides these there were exhibits of unusual birds and animals from tne mountains and oceans of other countries. We specially noticed a monkey over six feet tall and an exhibit of more than seven hundred species of snakes. There were many other things also but I shall not describe them.

There was a thunder storm of severe intensity about 2:00 P.M. It was as dark as night so that the lamps were lit in the houses. The thunder and rain soon ceased.

May 8th.                          Cloudy.

Since today is Sunday all the shops are closed as they were last Sunday. In this country gold, silver, and copper are used as coins and there is also much foreign money. It was decided today that we should return to Japan by the Cape of Good Hope.

May 9th.                          Clear.

At nine o'clock we went to a studio and had our photographs taken. It took only a few moments to take pictures of the six of us. The photographer had us sit in a chair and from the top of our heads to the sole of our feet we were not allowed to move, not even to wink an eye. If one moved even a little the photograph would not be clear. There were three lenses in the square box. This box rested on a tall stand. The photographic plate was made of glass painted with a silver mixture. After the picture was taken the photographic plate was removed in a dark room and washed in five different chemical solutions. When it dried the figure was very clear. The price of a picture varied from one half dollar to ten dollars.

The three chief commissioners went to the astronomical observatory at 5:00 P.M. Shortly after 10:00 P.M. there was a fire across the street from our hotel. When the fire alarm was sounded many people gathered. The people cried, " Fire ! Fire ! " in a loud voice. This is their way of giving the fire alarm. Only one house was burned before the fire was extinguished.

May 10th.                          Clear.

At five o'clock we went to a reception given by a member of the diplomatic corps and saw some 200 dancing girls perform. We were served delicious wine and cake. Even when several hundred people go to a theater or other gatherings they are quiet and orderly. Even on the streets we did not see any people quarreling.

May 11th.                              Clear.

In the hotel was a large dining room where about 300 people gathered for a banquet. The tables and stands were decorated with vases of flowers which cost from one to six or seven dollars a vase. Four men seated on a platform played stringed instruments like Japanese shamisen and the music sounded like them also. A Japanese flag was hung from the center of the wall to the rear of the stage, and an American flag was hung on each side of it. The guests gathered in front of the stage to drink wine. This banquet lasts for three days and is in honour of the safe arrival of the Japanese.

May 12th.                              Clear.

The daily crowd of sightseers came to the hotel. There was a thunder storm and rain about 1:00 P.M. Earthquakes are very rare in this country. Since the country was settled there has not been one severe earthquake in the east, though there have been some slight earthquakes in the west but even there they have not been severe enough to shake ornaments off shelves. It is said that earthquakes are very rare because there are no volcanoes, and further because as there is too much water and too little fire in the earth to cause them. Every evening many ladies gather at the hotel to dance and sing, accompanied by the accordion.

May 13th.                              Cloudy.

Every day from morning till night a crowd of children collect under the window of the hotel to scramble for money or a piece of paper which the Japanese may give them. It causes us much inconvenience and we dislike it.

It is said that small houses are not permitted because when they are not repaired and are seen by foreigners it is a disgrace to the country. There are no slums in this city; all the buildings are from 90 to 114 ft. tall. The streets are sixty feet wide. The class of people who would live in a small house in Japan rent a room in a hotel. The hotel prepares the meals and charges a set price for board. The guests who have their meals in their rooms are very few, but when the dinner bell is rung most of the guests go to the dining room for their meals. The meals cost from one dollar to two dollars and a half per day; hence there are very few permanent guests. There are two meals a day. In the evening tea is served. I did not see people eating at any other time. Wine and cake are served with the two meals. In the evening bread is eaten with the tea. The servants, fare consists of corn beef and bread. In the evening there was a fire in the neighbourhood which destroyed one house.

May 14th.                    Clear.

About 9:00 A.M. we went for a walk. When we went out of the hotel we received an identification check. Two guides always went with each party.

The three chief commissioners went to see an exhibition in the afternoon and were served cake and wine.

In the evening a negro played the piano and sang in a very peculiar voice. Many people came to hear him. He is an expert on the piano, it is said, but it was not in the least interesting to us. The piano is a musical instrument which produces a sound like a Japanese " Koto ".

There was a fire just after mid-night.

May 15th.          Cloudy. Afternoon Rain.

The chief commissioners accompanied by five escorts went horseback riding this morning at 8:00 o'clock. The American ladies are skillful horse women. They ride side saddle. One lady rode in front of the commissioners. If they went fast she did also, hence they were unable to pass her. The horses of this country are fat and strong and gentle. This is because they are geldings. Many of the American horses are dappled.

May 16th.                 Cloudy.

A photographer came to the hotel after 10:00 A·M. and took pictures of the chief commissioners. As the President wanted an official photograph to keep in memory of the visit of the Japanese commission, he sent this photographer.

There was a sudden thunder and hail storm about 2:00 P.M. The hail stones were about the size of a four ounce iron ball. In the evening there was a magic lantern show at the hotel. There were pictures of American and foreign scenery, customs, famous places, fires, electric storms, etc., which were greatly enlarged by magic lantern.

May 17th.                 Clear.

The chief commissioners went to bid good-bye to the President at noon. We went for a walk in the afternoon.

In the evening there was another magic lantern show at the hotel. The President unaccompanied by any aides escorted two or three ladies to the hotel to see the pictures. We were surprised to see the President so democratic.

May 18th.                 Clear.

While we stayed at the hotel we had the following things to eat : Wine, fruit, meat, fish, rice, things made of flour, coffee, eggs, sugar, butter, ice water, soup, yam, and nuts. The meat and fish were boiled in salt water or else fried, but were not salty. We ate these dishes very rarely. Salt, vinegar, sauce, mustard, pepper, etc. were always on the table. There were many flies but no mosquitoes or fleas. We saw few birds, least of all swallows and sparrows.

May 19th.                 Clear.

Because we are leaving tomorrow many people came at night to say good-bye. When we met them we all wept. Seeing them also weeping we realized that they are tender-hearted people. In the evening there was another magic lantern show. It is said that there are 10,000 houses in Washington and that the population is 60,000.

May 20th.                    Clear.

We left Washington this morning and came to Baltimore. We got in carriages at the hotel and drove about 1½ miles to the station. There we boarded the train. This train is like the one we rode in at Panama, though the coaches are a little larger so that they accommodate forty passengers. Soon after we got into the train it started and ran twice as fast as the Panama train. As the train was very noisy two passengers sitting next to each other could not carry on a conversation. The train passed quickly out of the city into the country. The landscape has no hills and valleys and is all flat. Here and there we saw houses among groves of trees. Much grass was growing in the fields. There were also cultivated fields but as the train went so fast I am not certain what was growing, but I think there were barley and corn. We saw pine, oak, cherry etc., along the way.

We arrived in Baltimore, Maryland. It is 36 miles from Washington to Baltimore. Carriages came up to the two stone arches in front of the station to meet us. We immediately got into them. The procession proceeded slowly along the street between two lines of spectators. About 400 soldiers armed with rifles guarded our route. They were assisted by 160 cavalrymen, three brass bands, and eight fire companies. They were equipped with a device for shooting water by steam pressure, fire axes, ladders, and cannon, with which they carefully guarded us.

The men pulled their hats and the ladies waved handkerchiefs to welcome us from the street and from the second, fourth, third, fifth, and sixth stories of the houses. Japanese flags and flags inscribed with " Great Japan " in Chinese characters were being waved by the spectators. On both sides of the street there were buildings of seven or eight stories like great mountains. Having proceeded about a mile we arrived at the arsenal where we stopped. Going up to the second story we rested. The hall was about $180 \times 120$ feet. A gallery runs all around the four walls. The hall was decorated with a profusion of flowers arranged on tables on both sides and at one end. We sat on a platform in the middle of the hall and saw several hundred ladies, and about two hundred soldiers drilling outside the building.

We went outside, got in carriages and proceeded to the hotel about 3:00 P.M. The hotel was like the hotel in Washington. A flag was flying above it. An entertainment was given near the hotel by the city firemen in our honour. There were eight companies, each of which had a pump. They pumped the water from a pond and shot it up about 120 feet. The water fell in every direction and looked like a cloud or mist. It came down upon the spectators like rain so that they scattered. Great confusion ensued, but as their clothes were made of wool they were not spoilt. The firemen's ladder was about 78 feet long but as it could be folded up it was quite easy to handle. About 500 soldiers drilled. There was a display of fireworks like Japanese fireworks, light blue and yellow, which were exploded high up in the air. Then there were other fireworks displayed on the ground.

In front of the hotel there was a large park about $720 \times 300$ feet, in which was a large statue in stone consisting of a human figure on each side of which was an eagle. This was a memorial of the war between England and America in which Washington fought. About twenty policemen stood guard at the entrance of the hotel. The policemen are chosen from among the strongest men in the country. The population of Baltimore is 300,000, it is said.

May 21st.                    Cloudy.

At 10:00 A.M. we went by carriage to the station from the hotel. As Baltimore is on the bank of a big river large ships come up to the very entrance of the doors of the buildings. Boarding the train after 10:00 o'clock we travelled north. The coaches were very fine. There were three coaches accommodating forty passengers each. The interior of the coaches was decorated with red and white bunting and Japanese flags. As I explained the speed before I shall not do so now. We passed through broad fields where houses were very scarce. The grass, trees, and forests were a lovely green. Having travelled about ten miles we came to a large river which was two miles wide in its broadest reaches and was crossed by a bridge about a mile long. About 12:00 after travelling several miles we came to a town near a broad river. This river flowed so fast that a bridge could not be built. Hence there was a ferry to carry over the train. The ferry boat decorated with flags of Japan and America waited for the train. The deck of the ferry was flat and was covered over by an iron roof. Very soon the train was run on to the tracks of the ferry and thus was ferried across the river. This was most interesting. On each side of the river the tracks on land are connected with the tracks on the ferry by a movable section of track which makes it possible for the train to run on and off the ferry whether the river is high or low. The ferry is built in a rectangular shape and is 360 feet by 60 feet. When the ferry arrived at the opposite bank of the river the movable section of track was lowered on to it, and the train ran off the ferry on to the track on the land immediately. After travelling about 10 miles we arrived at Wilmington, a city of 300 houses and many temples as seen from the train. Between the river and Wilmington there were many pine forests, and broad fields in which wheat, corn, barley, and beans were cultivated. Cows and hogs were feeding in the fields. We had lunch on the train consisting of beef, chicken, bread, and champagne.

It is twenty-eight miles from Wilmington to Philadelphia. We arrived in Philadelphia about 3:00 P.M. It is 99 miles from Baltimore to Philadelphia. It is about two-thirds of a mile from the city limits to the station. After arriving at the station we got into carriages and were escorted by 3,000 infantrymen armed with rifles and 1,000 cavalrymen carrying drawn swords. Their uniforms were very fine. There were about 2,000 policemen guarding the route. As I explained before, these men are selected from among the strongest in the country. Both sides of the street were so packed with people that every available space was taken. About forty of our escorts wore ribbons across their chests inscribed in Chinese characters which being interpreted mean "Welcome to our Japanese friends." Probably this inscription was written by a Chinese. All along the route, from the front window of each house, a Japanese flag inscribed with characters meaning, "Great Japan," and an American flag were hung. Here and there large Japanese flags were hung down from ropes suspended across the street; people waved small Japanese flags to us from the windows of the second, third, fourth, fifth and sixth stories of the houses on both sides of the street.

Those who did not have flags waved white handkerchiefs. The men waved their hats and shouted. From all directions people threw flowers into the carriages. This was like a festival. We arrived at the hotel about 5:00 P.M. Three hundred infantrymen and three hundred cavalrymen guarded the entrance of the hotel. In all the history of America never have so many guards been used before, it is said. This hotel is similar to those in Washington and other cities, but as it is a new one we were surprised at its elegance.

May 22nd.                    Clear.

The entire street was paved with large stones; the place for the carriages was in the middle. It is said that the most beautiful women in America live in Philadelphia. The rooms of this hotel are new and fine. Even our rooms had a closet and a connecting bath and toilet. It was very convenient to have hot and cold water on tap. As I gave a detailed description of the carpet on the floor of the bath and toilet in Washington I will not do so again. This hotel, "Continental Hotel," has 600 rooms.

In Philadelphia there are comparatively few small shops but many wholesale houses and rich men. Philadelphia is famous for its gold and silver smiths and glass factories.

May 23rd.                    Clear.

There was a fire just after six o'clock this morning. Many firemen rushed to the fire. There was an American and a Japanese flag on the fire wagon and small Japanese flags on the fire ladders. On each fire pump there was a Japanese and an American flag. The drays and the bridles of the horses were decorated with Japanese flags.

Every morning and evening the streets are watered. A large watertank built on a wagon has many small holes in it through which the water runs on to the street causing it to look as though there had been a rain. This is a convenient device.

In Washington and Philadelphia and all other American cities the mothers do not carry their babies on their backs or in their arms but put them in small baby carriages which are pushed by maidservants. The maidservants cause the children to play.

About 2:00 P.M. we went with the three chief commissioners to the city reservoir. There is a large river running at the foot of the hill on which the reservoir is built. When it is seen from a distance it is very beautiful. It is like Asukayama in the suburbs of Tokyo. There we had refreshments consisting of wine, cakes, bread, etc. There was a water wheel for raising the water into the reservoir from which it flowed by gravity into the city.

We went to a boiler factory; from there we returned to the hotel about 5 o'clock. Although it was about three miles from the hotel to the reservoir it took a very short time, as the carriage travelled fast.

There was a fire during the night.


May 24th.                    Clear.

Many people gathered in front of the hotel. Among them were three beautiful young ladies, and when we saw them we rushed for the window to shake hands with them scrambling for the first place. After we shook hands with them they went away and later came back bringing bouquets of beautiful flowers which they handed to the police and asked them to give them to the Japanese. When we received them we were surprised at their loveliness and asked how much they cost and learned that they were worth about one dollar. We gave each of the ladies our visiting cards. They received the cards joyfully and went away.

When we walked on the street or were in the hotel people came up, shook hands to welcome us, and went home very happy. We see by this conduct that the Americans respect the people of other countries.

In the afternoon we went to a theater to see a play. Though the acting was like the acting in Japanese plays yet the stage and galleries were different. There was a revolving stage and other theatrical apparatus on a large scale. The first scene that we saw showed a paramour talking to the wife of another. When he heard the footsteps of the husband returning home from the field he hid in a closet. The wife tried to get the husband to go away but he would not, so that she was very much worried. Although we did not understand the words, the acting was interesting to us.

In the next play a daughter of a rich man was talking on the street with her lover and planned that he should bring a ladder to her house so that he could get up to her room.  Another man standing near by in the shadow heard the engagement.  In the evening he carried a ladder to the appointed place but as it was dark could not find the window.  Later the lover came bringing his ladder.  But neither knew that the other was there.  In the dark they balanced their ladder against one another and each climbed up to the top.  There one took the hand of the other and kissed it.  Then both of them crashed to the ground where they had a terrific argument.  The lover lost the fight which ensued and was thrown into a well by the other man who fled.  In the morning when the heroine found the body of her lover she was greatly surprised.  She acted her part well.

In the next act the dancers were dressed in costumes the fronts of which were American and the backs of which were Japanese. They then fenced with spears and swords.  There was much more but I shall not describe it.

The female characters were acted by women who performed so well that we considered them more skilful than Ichikawa Kodanji, who was the most expert actor of female parts in Japan at his time.


May 25th.                 Clear.

In American hotels and in the homes of rich people china, glass, and silver ware are used.  The silver is very beautiful and economical.  If china or glass ware is broken it cannot be sold, but if silver ware is broken it can be sold for the value of the silver which it contains.  The price of gold and silver in America is higher than in Japan but both are used very much.  For example, some walking sticks have a gold or silver handle which is excessively luxurious.  The rich people change their underwear three times a day and even the poor people change their underwear once a day.  They do this because if their clothes get dirty they may become sick.  Even poor people go into their own bedroom and lock their door when they change their shoes and stockings.  Even the members of their own families do not see them.  When some one wishes to go into the room of another person he first knocks upon the door and if the occupant of the room says, "Come in!" he may then open the door and go in.

In each room there is a looking-glass and on a shelf in front of it there is a brush, comb, and hair oil. Even if a guest is going out of his room for a few minutes he looks into the mirror and if his hair is dishevelled he brushes it. I was surprised at how well groomed the people of this country are.

About 9:00 A.M. the chief commissioners went to a gold and silver smith's. About sundown a beautiful girl of 16 or 17 came to the window in front of the hotel. Some of our company gave her a Japanese print and paper from which Japanese fans are made and asked for her visiting card.

The other American girls took her gifts and ran away. Some man standing by pushed her over but a policeman stopped him and took her home. The other people were jealous because this one girl received so much from the Japanese. After that incident we could not give anything away. When the Americans threw presents into the second-story windows, we were forbidden to receive them.

May 26th.                    Clear.

At 9:00 A.M. the three commissioners and other members of the commission went to the United States Mint. Much gold and silver was stored there. Although I cannot describe it the process of minting the coins is most fascinating. The entire process is performed by machinery. The gold and silver kept in reserve for use during war looks like a mountain when one sees it stored in the strong room. We were amazed. We returned to the hotel about noon.

At the hotel there was a woman about 30 years of age who, though she was very fat and strong, was quite beautiful. She was able to lift a large incense burner which held about nine gallons. She was as strong as two or three ordinary men. Most Americans have strong arms.

Children from seven to eighteen years old carrying their books and tablets went to school and in the afternoon returned together.

Two or three American men came to our hotel. We gave them

Japanese paper. They were so pleased that they performed some tricks for us, which were not different from Japanese magic.

In the evening there was a magic lantern show at the hotel but as it was like that in Washington I shall not describe it.

There was a fire near the hotel about 2 o'clock in the morning.

May 27th.                        Clear.

In the afternoon we left the hotel and went to see a shop where paper flowers are made. The shop was decorated with many beautiful flowers made of paper. Many girls from 14 or 15 to 22 or 23 years old were making flowers in a room adjoining the shop. When we went into the room guided by the shop owner to where the girls were they all got up to welcome us. We gave each of them a visiting card and they seemed very pleased. Then the shop owner led us upstairs where many hats trimmed with artificial flowers were on display. Cake was served to us as we rested there. After a little while we went to a picture printing shop. The owner of this shop seeing us from a distance came to the front door to greet us and after shaking hands ushered us in and led us upstairs. Many workmen were printing pictures from copper plates. They worked with machinery. After watching this work for a few minutes we went into a waiting room which was fittied up with armchairs and other fine furniture. Here we were served champagne. We gave the proprietor some Japanese paper and a fan and he gave us a large printed picture.

When we were walking on the street a man asked us if we had seen the balloon. He insisted that we ride in his carriage with him. After going about one mile we arrived at the show ground which was surrounded on four sides by bleachers. About one hundred people who had gathered to see the balloon quickly diverted their attention to us as soon as they caught sight of us. It is said that the balloon is to fly from Philadelphia to New York today.

The balloon was made of a large bag painted with coal tar and filled with coal gas. The diameter was sixteen feet. Under the gas bag was a long tube. There was a net thrown over the gas bag which was attached to the basket below by many ropes. Below this was a heavy weight to anchor the balloon. The length of the basket shaped like a boat was six feet. Only one passenger could be carried in the basket. On the right and left sides of the basket there were Japanese and American flags· The balloon was taken near a small house about six feet square where coal gas was made. This coal gas was conveyed by an iron pipe to a rubber tubing which hung down from the gas bag. After the balloon left the ground it was caught by a wind and blown about one mile to the northeast. As it was very fast it passed out of sight.

Although it is a hundred miles to New York it only takes 30 minutes to make the trip, because the balloon is equipped with a steam engine, it is said. It would take the balloon about six days to make the trip from New York to Japan, and it would take a bullet about $4\frac{1}{2}$ days to travel the same distance.

As the balloon sometimes goes up very high where the atmosphere is so thin that the passenger dies, balloons are not used except in an emergency. This ascent was made for our special benefit. Although man is skilful enough to make a balloon which can go so fast, yet it is not often used.

There is a telegraph line between New York and Philadelphia over which messages are sent as fast as lightning.

This device is electrical, but I cannot describe it.

This city is lighted by coal gas. This coal gas is made on a large lot where the coal is burned and the gas is passed through water to extract the offensive odor. It then is forced through the gas pipes which are jointed to the street and house lamps.

About 1 1/3 miles from the gas plant is a race course covering about 2/3 of a mile. By the race track there is a tall building around which many beautiful flowers are cultivated. Men and women come here to drive in their carriages and to ride horseback. The American women are skilful horsewomen. We returned to the hotel about sundown.

About eight o'clock in the evening sixty companies of firemen paraded by the hotel with their fire pumps decorated with flowers. The firemen wore Japanese costumes and wigs and as they marched by shot off Roman candles.. There were some 3,000 firemen and several hundred musicians in the bands. The fireworks reflected in the windows made the streets as bright as day. The shouts of the spectators resounded like thunder. Although balls of fire shot through the air the spectators who wore hats and woollen clothes did not fear them. The procession which was about three miles long was so spectacular that I am unable to describe it.

May 28th.                    Cloudy.

Leaving the hotel about 9:00 A.M. we went in carriages a distance of one mile and a third to the Delaware River. There we took a steam ferry across the river which is about 2/3 of a mile wide and, arriving on the opposite bank, continued our journey in a train which was waiting for us. After making a run of 35 miles we arrived at Ambay about noon, where we embarked on a steam boat. Several hundred soldiers and thirty girls between 13 or 14 and 17 or 18 wearing boys' clothes and carrying Japanese flags saw us off. As soon as we started we had lunch on board ship. This is a bay and the waves are very high. We passed between Long Island and Staten Island which are about 2/3 of a mile apart. The scenery is very beautiful. The fortress on each island and the American battle-ships fired a salute as our boat sailed by. When we arrived at the Battery in New York eight cannons fired a salute. We landed at 2:00 P.M. and got into carriages. We were escorted by several thousand soldiers; and policemen carrying sticks about three feet long walked on both sides of our carriages. The spectators carrying flags and waving handkerchiefs or hats welcomed us. Some climbed up on stone fences or trees. But as it was like our Philadelphia welcome I shall not describe it.

After riding about one mile we stopped at a drill ground where we saw 2,000 American cavalrymen, 3,000 American infantrymen, and many British, French and Dutch soldiers drilling. The total number was 10,000. Each company was equipped with a different uniform. There was a band attached to each battalion. The soldiers marched in perfect step to the music. Three nurses equipped with knapsacks about one foot square filled with medicine and bandages marched with each company.

Riding about one mile and a third we arrived at the hotel. This is the largest hotel which we have seen since leaving Washington. This is a seven-story building and is surrounded by a spacious garden. Japanese and American flags hung down from each of the several hundred windows of the hotel.   A lantern made of five colors hung down from each window.   These lanterns were lit each evening.   The interior of the hotel was beautiful.   The owner of this hotel had several other hotels also, including the one in which we lodged in Philadelphia.   The shop keepers declared a holiday so as to welcome us today.

May 29th.                     Clear.

This harbour is busy and famous in America.   Every day from morning until night carriages and wagons pass along the street. There is a street light in front of each door which when lighted at night makes the street seem as bright as day.   Some buildings have as many as a hundred gas lights over the entrance.   The light in the rooms of the houses shining through the glass windows at night is so wonderful and is such a surprise to us that I cannot describe it.   After sundown men and women walking on the streets create lively sights.   Because many people from other countries live in New York we were heavily guarded when we went out.   As we came to America people of other countries were jealous.   If any accident should happen to us the Americans would be responsible.

June 1st.                     Clear.

At one o'clock the three chief commissioners went to the City Hall.   They were escorted by a forty-piece brass band, thirty cavalrymen carrying sabers and five hundred infantrymen.   They returned to the hotel about 3:00 P.M.   During the day and night many soldiers armed with rifles marched in order to guard us. This is the Metropolitan Hotel on Broadway.

June 2nd.                     Clear.

Shortly after one o'clock there was a thunder storm.   About 2:00 P.M. we went for a walk.   In the evening we saw a play at the hotel performed by a negro minstrel.   The stage was larger than the usual Japanese stage.   It was equipped with a revolving stage and other theatrical apparatus.

In the play a robber kidnapped a beautiful lady and carried her to his den in a mountain fastness where he drank whiskey and made love to her. But she would not listen to his entreaties and manifested her distress by continually weeping.

During the intermission the spectators went out to drink wine and eat cake but came back to their seats before the beginning of the next act. But strange as it seemed to us, they did not eat or drink during the performance. The spectotors looked at us rather than at the play and those who were far away observed us through their opera glasses.

June 3rd.                          Clear.

Again there was a thunder storm in the afternoon. We went to see another play today also. The players used Japanese costumes. In the evening we saw another negro ministrel at the hotel. We were invited to many theaters because many people crowded to the hotel to see us. The theater managers realized that if the Japanese went to their theaters more people would be attracted thither.

The manager of the Metropolitan Hotel was a colonel in the Russian army during the Crimean War and commanded 300 cavalry and 2,000 infantry and was an officer of great merit.

June 4th.                          Clear.

We went to the botanical gardens at one o'clock. The gardens cover about eighty acres. They consist of many trees and flowers planted about artificial hills and around a lovely pond into which eight streams flow. The scenery is so beautiful that I cannot describe it. We noticed one especially large fine needle pine tree. It is said that the botanical gardens cost about $20,000,000.00. We ate refreshments consisting of wine and cake and saw many beautiful girls dancing.

June 5th.                          Clear.

After six o'clock we went up on the roof garden and looked

at the moon and stars through a telescope. The surface of the moon looked as if it were covered with many balls of oil. We saw the evening star which looked like the crescent moon, and several other stars of various shapes.

June 6th.                    Clear.

After eight o'clock in the morning we went for a walk. We attended a circus where we saw several bears larger than cows wrestling and climbing trees. We saw yellow pigeons and tigers and other animals.

June 7th.                    Clear.

Because today is Sunday all of the shops are closed. As we were so well guarded while in New York we gave $20,000.00 to the authorities. On account of this gift we have a good reputation here.

June 8th.                    Clear.

Carpenters and gardeners began yesterday to prepare for the banquet and dance which was for our entertainment in the evening. They worked all last night and only finished at sundown. They built a new stage 300 × 180 ft. on which 6,000 dancing girls performed. Many ladies and gentlemen came to the dance and feasted at banquet tables arranged here and there near the stage. The garden was beautified by many flowers and the light which shone upon them from thousands of lanterns. We were amazed at the brilliance. We drank wine and danced with the Americans through the night until break of day.

June 9th.                    Clear.

It is very hot today. At one o'clock in the afternoon we accompanied our chief commissioners to the home of Commodore Perry who went to Japan several years ago. Commodore Perry became sick and died some time ago but his adopted son was at home. The home was very fine and was decorated with many Japanese mementoes and pictures of Commodore Perry taken in Japan. We were entertained with wine and cake. Two Japanese spaniels in the house sniffed our clothes and realizing that we were Japanese danced at our feet, leaped in our laps and chewed our sleeves and would not leave us. While Commodore Perry was in Japan he bought these dogs and brought them back to his home, where they have lived ever sinee. They loved us as soon as they saw us and when we departed they followed us, and though they could not speak they had feelings like men. They showed their affection so plainly for us by their voice that we were quite sad and shed a tear when we left them.

Leaving the Perry home we rode in carriages about ½ mile to a large house, where we met several hundred ladies and gentlemen and were served with refreshments of wine and cake.

About 3:00 P.M. we saw a balloon, but as I described one before I shall not repeat. It passed over head so fast that we scarcely had time to see it. People are usually prohibited from riding in balloons and any one who goes up in a balloon is considered very foolish.


June 10th.                    Clear.

In the afternoon we all went for a walk. One American took us by the hand and led us with him rather against our will as we did not understand what he intended to do. He took us to a show given by a magician. On the stage were many boxes and other apparatus used in the performance. There were many lights in the hall. Two Americans came on the stage and after a few introductory remarks began their show. They were skilful and held our attention.


June 12th.                    Clear.

In the morning we went for a walk. In all the cities of America there are not only primary schools but schools of higher grade also. There are schools for the deaf, dumb, and blind. The deaf and dumb are taught by means of pictures which are inscribed with a legend of explanation. The teacher by means of the pictures and gestures teaches the class. The blind are taught by means of raised letters impressed in paper. As the government pays for the schools the students do not pay. There are other schools for foundlings and orphans. There is another institution called a hospital in which paupers and those who have no relatives to take care of them are placed when they are sick and cannot buy their own medicine. Many doctors and nurses care for the patients in the hospitals.

This city is thirteen miles long and six miles wide. The population is 3,000,000.

June 12th.                    Clear.

We left the hotel in carriages this morning at 10:00 o'clock. After driving about 2 miles we arrived at the water front where we boarded a launch and embarked on a frigate after going about a mile in the launch.

The length of the frigate was 350 feet and her width 50 feet. It was equipped with two copper funnels nine feet in diameter. She carried many cannon.

We were quartered in the stern in new but small cabins. Our cabin was only six feet square and eleven people had to sleep in it. After our baggage was gotten aboard refreshments of wine and cake were served. The soldiers drilled on deck. The appearance of the interior of this ship was like the " Powhatan," hence I shall not try to describe it. We remained on the ship in the harbour today. Many large ships were in the harbour. Among them was the British warship " Great Western." She is 680 feet long and is equipped with six masts and five funnels. She is said to be the largest ship afloat and was sent to America by the Queen so that the Japanese could see it. There was a thunder storm at 2:00 P.M. Since we landed in America all our food was western style and flavored with salt and we did not have bean mash or soy. While we stayed in the hotel in New York we saw a theatrical each evening. Every day there was a fire in New York.

June 13th.                    Clear.

The anchor was raised at noon and we sailed east. After
proceeding two miles we saw forts on land on both sides. As we
sailed by, the forts fired a salute. At 2:00 P.M. we passed Sandy
Hook from which point the pilot boat returned. The sailors
climbed the rigging and in a loud voice called good-bye to the
pilot as the boats sailed apart.

# DIARY OF VOYAGE

## Volume III

June 15th.                      Clear.                      North Wind.

The warship on which we are riding is called the "Niagara."
It was so named by the niece of the President. This is the name
of a waterfall in America, the largest in the world.

    Latitude      N. 39° 26'.
    Longitude     W. 66° 26'.
    Temperature   72° F.


June 29th.                      Clear.

We saw St. Anthony Island at noon and arrived at St.
Vincent at six o'clock.

    Latitude      N. 17½°.
    Longitude     W. 25°.
    Temperature   78° F.


July 21st.                      Cloudy.                      Southeast Wind.

We saw land on our right after 10:00 A.M. and anchored in
St. Paul de Loanda harbour at 5:00 P.M. The harbour is guarded
by a fort on the right.

    Latitude      S. 8° 20'.
    Longitude     E. 13° 01'.
    Temperature   72° F.


August 11th.                      Cloudy.

In morning West wind. In afternoon East Wind.
    In the afternoon we sighted the Cape of Good Hope.
    Latitude      S. 35° 18'.
    Longitude     E. 18° 36'.
    Temperature   67° F.

August 14th.                    Cloudy.

In the afternoon we sighted Christmas Island.
Latitude          S. 10° 58'.
Longitude        W. 105° 25'.
Temperature    80° F.


August 25th.                    Cloudy.              Southeast Wind.

We arrived at Batavia at 10:00 A.M.    As we had not eaten
Japanese food for 250 days we were delighted to have some " shoyu "
(sauce) on fish.    When we ate it we felt as though we  were home
again.


September 10th.                    Clear.                    East Wind.

We arrived in Hongkong.    There is a war going on between
China and Great Britain.


September 20th.                    Clear.                    North Wind.

On the left we sighted mountains on the island of Formosa.
This island is 245 miles from North to South and 100 miles from
East to West.    The population is 2,500,000.
Latitude          N. 22° 11'.
Longitude        E. 120° 15'.
Temperature    83° F.


September 24th.                    Cloudy.                    North Wind.

We saw an island off Satsuma Province in Japan.
Latitude          N. 28° 20'.
Longitude        E. 130° 38'·
Temperature    74° F.


September 26th.                    Clear.                    North Wind.

About sundown we sighted Mt. Asama in the Province of Ise.

Latitude       N. 33° 38'.
Longitude      E. 136° 28'.
Temperature    65° F.

September 28th.              Clear.

We saw the sails of many fishing boats glistening in the
morning sun.   A more beautiful scene we have not beheld in any
country.  Even the Americans on the ship praised this as the most
beautiful scenery in the world.  We arrived at Yokohama at noon,
where two or three persons landed, but the ship sailed to Shinagawa ;
the anchor was cast about 3:00 P.M.  We remained on board ship
until morning.

September 29th.              Clear.

We dressed in Japanese kimono and waited for the Japanese
ship which was coming to meet us.  This ship came about 8:00
A.M.  She saluted.  We landed, ate lunch, and walked into Yedo.

# MEMBERS OF THE MISSION

Members of the Embassy who went on board the American ship "Powhatan":—

Niimi Buzennokami Masaoki  (40)  [Head of Deputation]
  Misaki Tsukasa Yoshimichi  (35)
  Arai Mitsugi Sadakazu  (31)
  Sayama Hachiro Takasada  (24)
  Yasuda Zeniehiro Tamemasa  (37)
  Horiuchi Shogo Tomoharu  (17)
  Yanagawa Kanesaburo Masakiyo  (25)  [Diarist]
  Araki Kazuemon Yoshikatsu  (27)
  Tamamushi Sadayu Norishige  (36)
  Nichida Senzo  (40)

Muragaki Awajinokami Norimasa  (48)
  Takahashi Morinosuke Tsuneharu  (45)
  Nonomura Ichinoshin Tadazane  (44)
  Nishimura Ogoro Nagatada  (35)
  Yoshikawa Kinjiro Tadanobu  (16)
  Ayabe Shingoro Yukisuke  (37)
  Matsuyama Kichijiro Yoshinori  (58)
  Fukumura Isokichi Muneaki  (42)
  Tani Bunichiro Fumikazu  (35)
  Suzuki Iwajiro Kanenori  (23)

Oguri Bungonokami Tadasu.
  Yoshida Kozo Nobunari  (35)
  Tsukamoto Mahiko Tsutomu  (29)
  Ebata Yuzo Hisakata  (29)
  Miyoshi Gonzo Yoshimichi  (24)
  Fukushima Keizaburo Yoshikoto  (19)
  Mimura Hirojiro Hidekiyo  (17)
  Kimura Tetsuta Kazunao  (31)
  Sato Toshiichi Nobunari  (54)
  Kimura Asazo Masayoshi  (26)

Morita Okataro Kiyoyuki  (49)

Hirose Kakuzo Kaneoki   (50)
Ishikawa Kwankichi Katsumi   (35)
Kano Shozo Sadayasu   (34)
Miura Tozo Michikata   (34)
Gomi Yasuemon Harumoto   (61)

Naruse Zenshiro Masanori   (39)
Hojo Genzo Akira   (32)
Yamada Umajiro Kiyoki   (30)
Hirano Shinzo   (30)

Tsukahara Jugoro Masayoshi   (36)
Motojima Hachiro Yoshinori   (30)
Yamura Sanosuke Katsutake   (29)

Hidaka Keizaburo Tameyoshi   (24)
Ito Kyuzaburo Kazutsura   (23)
Hirohara Kumazo Harutaka   (28)

Katabe Tetsutaro Masayoshi   (29)
Sato Yeizo Masayuki   (32)
Koike Senjiro Mitsuyoshi   (29)

Matsumoto Sannojo Harufusa   (30)
Ohama Gennosuke Hajime   (22)

Yoshida Sagoemon Hisamichi   (40)
Kishi Yahei Shigemitsu   (31)

Masuzu Ayajiro Masatoshi   (32)
Sano Kanae Sakari   (30)

Tsuji Yoshigoro Nobuaki (30)
Nakamura Shinkuro Nobuaki   (27)

Shiozawa Hikojiro   (34)
Kimura Dennosuke Masamori   (28)

Kurishima Hikoshiro Shigeyasu   (49)
Sakamoto Yasuta Yasuyoshi   (20)

Namura Gohachiro   (34)

Tateishi Tokujiro   (32)

Tateishi Fujiro Noriyuki   (17)
Katayama Tomokichi Taketomi   (27)

Miyazaki Tatemoto Masayoshi   (34)
Soito Goichiro Tadazane   (30)

Murayama Osamoto Atsushi  (32)
     Ohashi Ozo Takamichi  (50)

Kawasaki Michitami Tsutomu  (30)
     Shimauchi Yeinosuke Kanetaka  (28)

*Members for foreign affairs :—*
    Okada Heisaku
    Yamamoto Kisaburo  (49)
    Kato Motonari  (32)
    Sato Junzo  (37)
    Iino Bunzo  (35)

  Servant  Hanjiro  (55)
     Tetsugoro  (22)

  Total . . . . . . . . . . . . 77

Names of the crew and passengers of the Japanese Warship
" Kwanrin-maru " :—

| | |
|---|---|
| The Secretary of Naval Affairs . . . | Kimura Settsunokami |
| Commander in Chief . . . . . . | Katsu Rintaro |
| Instructor . . . . . . . . . . | Sakura Aitaro |
| „ . . . . . . . . . . | Suzuki Yujiro |
| „ . . . . . . . . . . | Nakamura Manjiro |
| „ . . . . . . . . . . | Ono Tomogoro |
| „ . . . . . . . . . . | Matsuoka Kinjiro |
| Assistant . . . . . . . . . . | Nezu Kinjiro |
| „ . . . . . . . . . . | Okada Izo |
| „ . . . . . . . . . . | Komatsu Gonnoshin |
| „ . . . . . . . . . . | Akamatsu Daisaburo |
| Engineer . . . . . . . . . . | Yamamoto Ojiro |
| „ . . . . . . . . . . | Ban Tetsutaro |
| „ . . . . . . . . . . | Hida Hamagoro |
| The Section of General Affairs . . . | Yoshioka Yuhei |
| | Konagai Gohachiro |
| Rotainers of the Kimura House . . . | Nagao Kosaku |
| | Saito Tomezo |
| | Hideshima Tonosuke |
| | Fukuzawa Yukichi |
| | Ohashi Eiji |

    Other Japanese . . . . . . . . 93
      Americans . . . . . . . . 11

# INFORMATION

The coal to be spent in the voyage from Yokohama to San Francisco is about 800 tons. A ton is equal to our 120 "Kin." The "Powhatan" is said to use 33 tons of coal per day.

From Yedo to Sandwich Islands ............................. 3145 American "Ri"

From Yedo to San Francisco .................................... 4800      "

From Sandwich Islands to San Francisco .................. 2130      "

From San Francisco to Panama............................... 3450      "

From Panama to Aspenwal (Land route) .................. 57      "
    (The Steam Car is used in this route)

From Aspenwal to Washington ................................ 1760      "

From Washington to New York................................ 200 American "Ri"
    (It takes 8 hours by steam-car on this route)

From Washington to Boston .................................... 440      "
    (It takes 18 hours by steam-car on this route)

From New York to Boston ....................................... 200      "

From San Francisco to Acapulco ............................. 2000      "
    (This is a port situated between San Francisco and Panama. It is about 4690 "Ri" from our Shimoda Port in Izu to the Capital of Sandwich Islands.)

Capital of America...............Washington.

Capital of England..............London.

Capital of Holland..............Amsterdam.

Capital of Russia ..............St. Petersburg.

（此所 バーペスヌニ・ドツテーレトトスライ・ズリスレ・クンラフ）圖峯到頓盛華節使華米遣

The Japanese Deputation Arrives in Washington, D.C.

*(From Frank Leslie's Illustrated Newspaper)*

（遣米節使大統領會見所圖（ワシントン、ホールスル、トライ、ドウテー、ニューベ、ーバー所繪））

The Japanese Mission Interviewing President Buchanan.

*(From Frank Leslie's Illustrated Newspaper)*

三月
晦日ニ
シテ丁ト
庭上眺
望之圖

Garden Viewed from
President's Room
on the last day of March

Tower for
a lamp at
night

鳴檣
夜八常登

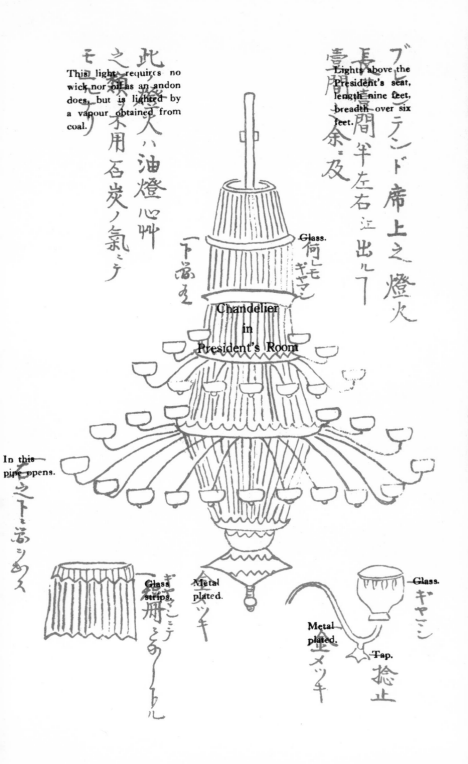